# Spray
# Finishing

# Spray
# Finishing

ANDY CHARRON

The Taunton Press

Cover photo: Boyd Hagen

BOOKS & VIDEOS

*for fellow enthusiasts*

© 1996 by The Taunton Press, Inc.
All rights reserved.

First printing: 1996
Printed in the United States of America

A FINE WOODWORKING Book

FINE WOODWORKING® is a trademark of the Taunton Press, Inc.,
registered in the U.S. Patent and Trademark Office.

The Taunton Press, 63 South Main Street, Box 5506, Newtown,
CT 06470-5506

Library of Congress Cataloging-in-Publication Data

Charron, Andy.
    Spray finishing / Andy Charron.
    p.     cm.
    "A Fine woodworking book" —
    Includes index.
    ISBN 1-56158-114-3
    1. Wood finishing.   2. Spray painting.       I. Title.
TT325.C495 1996
684'.084—dc20                                          96-33748
                                                       CIP

## About Your Safety

Working wood is inherently dangerous. Using hand or power tools improperly or
ignoring standard safety practices can lead to permanent injury or even death. Don't
try to perform operations you learn about here (or elsewhere) unless you're certain
they are safe for you. If something about an operation doesn't feel right, don't do it.
Look for another way. We want you to enjoy the craft, so please keep safety foremost
in your mind whenever you're in the shop.

For my wife Anne, whose steadfast support has made this all possible.

# ACKNOWLEDGMENTS

This book could not have been written without the help of a number of people. Some willingly lent me a hand along the way, while others unknowingly played a significant role in educating me about spray finishing and woodworking in general.

First, I would like to thank the following people from The Taunton Press: Jim Chiavelli and Helen Albert for all they did to make my idea a reality; Joanne Renna for her help and patience; Ruth Dobsevage, whose astute editorial direction helped shape this book; and Alec Waters, who gave me the courage to pursue this idea in the first place.

Thanks also go to Chip Carosia, of Einrosia Photography, for his professionalism, attention to detail and willingness to adapt to my ever-changing schedule.

Several manufacturer's representatives played a great role in providing helpful and timely information about their products and equipment. I would like to thank the following individuals and companies for their help: Tim Fondy and DeVilbiss Spray Booth Products; Bill Boxer and Apollo Sprayers Inc.; Nancy Specht, Dan Zimmerman and AccuSpray; Mike Bunnell and Can-Am; Chrissy Bertolini and Chemco Manufacturing Corp.; Daryl Arnold and Dispo, Inc.; Herb Oughton, Alphonso Fernandez and Binks Manufacturing Co.; Lon McCloskey, Lisa Spencer and Wagner Spray Tech Corp.; and Kristen Scutella and Ingersoll-Rand. Finally, a special note of thanks to Loren Simonson and DeVilbiss Industrial Coating Equipment for going above and beyond the call of duty.

I would also like to thank three people who have, without realizing it, helped me along the way. These include Chris Minick, whose writings are a constant source of help and information as I work my way through the often mysterious world of finishing; Bruce Nevad, who patiently taught me the basics of spray finishing and continues to be a source of inspiration; and especially Bob Grause, for getting me into this business in the first place.

Finally, I would like to say a special thanks to my son Brian for his help on the computer and to my father, who taught me at an early age the joy of working with wood.

# CONTENTS

# INTRODUCTION

Several years ago I was remodeling someone's kitchen and I managed to put a rather large and noticeable scratch on the face of a brand-new cabinet. I had two options. I could send the damaged cabinet back to the shop for refinishing, or I could repair it myself. The custom shop that built the cabinet was a three-hour drive away and wanted a fair sum of money to refinish the cabinet, so I decided to do it myself. The manufacturer told me the exact mix of stain and the brand of nitrocellulose lacquer he used, so I figured, how hard could it be? The first hint that I was headed for trouble came as I was purchasing the lacquer. I asked the salesman if there were any special instructions or precautions I should take.

He said, "That depends. What type of system are you using, air or airless?" Unsure of what he meant, I thought for a second before responding. I didn't own any spray equipment so I was sure I wasn't going to be using an air system. Since I was going to be using a brush to apply the lacquer I concluded the "system" I would use must obviously be airless.

"Airless," I responded with a certain amount of confidence.

"With an airless system you may need to thin the lacquer about 5%, depending on your equipment, the temperature and humidity," replied the salesman.

"Okay, sure," I said as I was handed a can of the appropriate thinner. So far so good. "What type of brush do you recommend I use?"

"Brush?" he asked. "Why do you need a brush? You can't brush this stuff, it has to be sprayed!"

I could tell by the incredulous look on the salesman's face that I was in more trouble than I thought. "You said airless, so I thought..." By now I was mumbling, and I had a sinking feeling in my stomach. "But I don't even own a spray gun," I finally managed to blurt out.

"No problem," came the reassuring reply. "We rent spray systems. I'll have you set up in no time."

It took me about three days of trial and error, along with a dozen or so calls to the paint store, but I finally got a passable finish on that cabinet. Thus began my education in the world of spray finishing.

This first adventure whet my appetite to learn more about finishing in general and spraying in particular. Coincidentally, I happened to be looking for an alternative to the hand-rubbed oil I was using at the time, and it wasn't long before I began to consider investing in HVLP (high-volume, low-pressure) spray equipment. The efficiency, ease and speed of application, combined with the quality and different types of finish that can be used, made the purchase of a spray system inevitable. Before spending any money, I decided to prepare myself as well as possible by looking into both compressed-air and HVLP systems and checking out a number of brands and manufacturers. Although I had done only that one repair job, I wasn't too concerned. After all, I assumed the gun would come with complete instructions that would make the learning process quick and easy.

Much to my chagrin, however, the equipment came with a brief pamphlet that contained general advice covering the basic operation of the system, but no hints or tricks that might help turn a merely decent spray job into a truly professional one. Numerous calls to spray-gun manufacturers and conversations with professional painters and finishers, combined with a lot of trial and error, helped me feel my way through the ins and outs of spray finishing. I quickly realized that although the information on spray finishing is available to anyone willing to spend time sifting through mounds of material, it is not always easy to find or there when you need it in a hurry. Hence the concept for this book.

There are plenty of books on how to finish furniture, and most have sections on spray finishing, but none of them devotes more than a few pages of general information to the subject. So I decided to compile the available information into one handy reference work that is complete and easy to use. The purpose of this book is to explain in clear, easy-to-follow terms how spray systems work and how to use them, focusing on HVLP guns, which are fast replacing earlier types of spray equipment. The book begins with a discussion of the pros and cons of spraying finishes. Then we take a look at the equipment available and why you would use it, in an effort to help first-time purchasers choose the best equipment for their own needs. The next chapter will help you set up the system in your shop. Included are discussions of different types of spray booths, spray rooms, compressors and safety equipment. Subsequent chapters follow the same order you would follow when spraying a piece: thinning and straining the material, setting up and adjusting the gun properly and actual spray techniques. Discussions of different materials and how to use them are followed by a look at specialty applications such as shading and toning. The last chapter covers cleaning and maintaining your spray system. The book concludes with a troubleshooting reference chart, three typical spray schedules and a glossary of terms.

Whether you are a novice who has no real knowledge of spray finishing or an experienced painter or cabinetmaker, I hope that this book will provide you with the information you need and become a handy reference for quickly finding specific and detailed answers to immediate problems. Above all, it is my aim to uncover the mysteries that surround spray finishing by showing you how easy it is to achieve perfect sprayed finishes time after time, with as little effort and as few problems as possible.

# CHAPTER 1

# To Spray or Not to Spray

When I first began professional woodworking I operated out of a one-car garage. Most of what little space I had was filled with a table saw, a jointer, a drill press and a workbench. Needless to say, working quarters were tight, so only those tools that were absolutely necessary to produce custom furniture found a place in the shop. There was no room for a dust-collection system or a separate finishing room. As a result, getting a good, dust-free finish with brushed-on, evaporative coatings was difficult and often frustrating. It seemed that no matter how thoroughly I cleaned the shop, dust always settled into the freshly applied finish. This created the need for a lot of sanding and recoating. Although I was usually able to get pretty good results, I was never really satisfied with the procedure and the outcome.

After several frustrating attempts at brushing on varnish, I realized that I would have to come up with a better method for finishing my work. Given the limitations of my shop, oil was the obvious alternative. Soon all of my pieces were being finished with hand-rubbed oil of one kind or another. Oil finishes offer many advantages over varnish or shellac. They are extremely easy to apply and don't require any special equipment. You simply wipe them on, wait a while and wipe off the excess. Since an oil finish doesn't build a thick surface film, as varnish or lacquer does, you don't have to worry about dust, lint or any other stray particles getting trapped in the finish. As a result, oil can be applied just about anywhere under less than ideal conditions. Although you should always have good ventilation when working with

**Oil finishes are easy to apply and are ideal for dusty shops that don't have adequate ventilation for spray equipment.**

any finish material, you don't need a separate finish area or spray booth when working with oil finishes. In my case, I simply opened up the garage door in the summer or cracked a window and turned on a fan in the winter.

I also found that once a surface was properly prepared, the results obtained from wiping on an oil finish were consistent and reliable. Also, lighting was not as critical as it would have been when brushing on and sanding or rubbing out varnish. In my poorly lit, unheated, dusty garage, hand-rubbed oil seemed to be the perfect solution to my finishing problems. Fortunately, I have always liked the warm, soft glow of an oil finish, and the phrase "authentic, hand-rubbed finishes" soon became a key element in my marketing strategy.

Despite the fact that oil appeared to be the perfect material for my small shop, it did have drawbacks. First, the amount of protection offered by an oil finish is minimal when compared to most varnishes and lacquers. Also, an oil finish needs more maintenance than other top coats, especially when applied to items that see heavy use, such as a tabletop or chair. Since the oil is absorbed into the wood, surface imperfections such as sanding scratches tend to stand out more than they would under a film of lacquer or varnish. As a result, surface preparation when using oil becomes critical.

Finally, depending on temperature and humidity, a good oil finish can take several days to apply, and involves a great deal of wiping and rubbing. During those first few years as I began to establish my business, I usually had more time than paying customers, so I didn't always mind the extra work and hours spent on an oil finish.

As my business grew, I was able to purchase more equipment and move to a larger shop. As my workload increased, I began to notice that it was taking me longer to finish a piece than it did to make it. Although the oil finishes looked great, the time spent wiping and waiting for coats to dry was beginning to slow down production. I also found that most of my customers were not particularly thrilled with the idea of having to maintain the finished piece themselves. They wanted something that not only looked good but could also withstand a little abuse or neglect.

It soon became obvious that the only way I was going to turn a profit was to alter my finishing methods. Even though I added a separate finishing room and a dust-collection system to my shop, I knew that switching back to brush-on varnish would pose many of the same problems associated with oil. Slow drying and labor intensive, it was never really an option. I needed to find a method that was quick and would give consistently top-quality, low-maintenance finishes.

The obvious alternative was to invest in spray equipment.

## Advantages of spray finishing

Applying finishes with a spray gun offers several advantages over wiping or brushing. These include ease of repair, speed, versatility, control, simplicity and consistency of application.

**Spray finishes are forgiving.** Because a sprayed finish is built up in thin layers, small scratches and blemishes are not as obvious as they would be with an oil finish. Surface preparation, although important, doesn't require the time or effort needed to achieve a good oil finish.

**Spraying is fast.** Finish can be sprayed on pieces of any size or shape much faster than could ever be done with a brush or rag. If you have the proper setup, a coat of finish can be applied to 30 stools or 1,000 small wooden blocks in an hour. Also, because the finish material is "atomized," or broken into small particles by a stream of air, it dries very quickly. In fact, most sprayed lacquers, varnishes and water-based products dry to the touch in a matter of minutes and can be sanded and recoated in an hour or two. This makes spraying a superior finishing method for two reasons. First, multiple coats of fast-

**Spraying is fast. With a compressed-air HVLP gun, a coat of water-based lacquer was applied to all four sides and both ends of the 224 workbench legs pictured here in about two hours. Imagine doing the same job with a brush or rag!**

Just about any finish that can be applied with a brush or a rag can be sprayed: paint, stains, shellac, varnish, lacquers, water-based products and even contact cement.

drying material can be applied in one day, which helps make the entire process of setting up, spraying and cleaning up very efficient. Second, because a sprayed finish dries so fast, any dust in the air has little time to settle on the finished piece, thereby reducing or even eliminating the need for sanding between coats.

**Spraying is versatile.** Any finish that can be applied by brush or rag can be sprayed, but not all finishes that can be sprayed can be brushed or wiped. Having access to a spray system will open the door to an entire world of finishes that would otherwise be unavailable. Nitrocellulose lacquers and many water-based products are just a few of the finishes that should only be sprayed. In addition, a spray gun allows you to use many special techniques, such as shading and toning, that cannot be executed effectively by hand. In fact, a good spray system is so versatile you can even use it to spray contact cement, which is a great time-saver if you do a lot of laminate work.

**Spray guns give you greater control.** If you have your gun properly adjusted and use the right techniques, you will have excellent control over how and where the finish is applied. Although a spray gun has a lower transfer efficiency rate than a brush (65% to 90% for HVLP spray guns versus nearly 100% for a brush), you can control the rate of application and thickness of coats much better. Adjusting the air

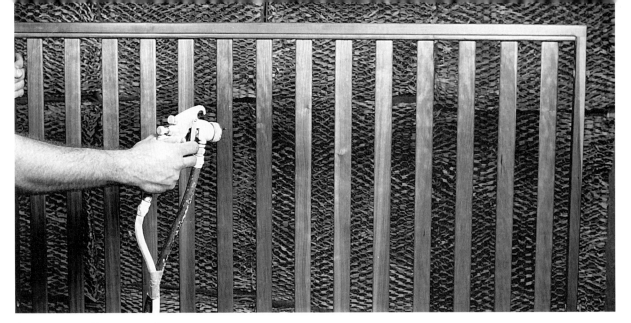

**Spray guns allow you to lay down an even coating over an entire piece, whatever its shape.**

pressure, fluid flow and fan size will allow you to apply light and even coats over the entire surface of the workpiece with no thick spots or brush marks.

**Spraying is easy to learn.** Despite what most people may think, the basics of using a spray gun are not hard to master. In fact, I have found that it takes less time to achieve an acceptable level of proficiency with a spray gun than it does with a brush. Stains and dyes can be applied quickly and evenly with uniform coverage and depth of color, giving your projects a more professional look.

**Spraying offers quality finishes on a consistent basis.** Without a doubt, the best reason for investing in a spray system lies in the quality of the finish. Spraying eliminates most of the problems associated with applying a finish by hand. Brush marks are no longer a problem, and the amount of dust in the air becomes less significant. Problems usually associated with brushing, such as runs, drips, sags and trapped air bubbles, are greatly reduced or even eliminated. When properly set up, used and maintained, a spray system will give you a smooth, high-quality and durable finish in a fraction of the time it would take to get the same results with a brush or rag.

## Other considerations

As attractive as spray finishing seems, it has a few drawbacks. First, setting up a system that is safe and will operate efficiently may take a lot of shop space and will certainly cost a fair amount of money. In ad-

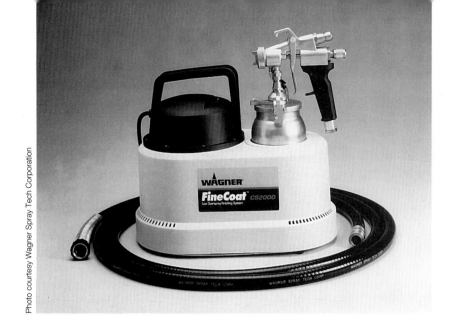

**Spray systems do not have to be large or expensive. A compact, two-stage (HVLP) turbine/gun unit offers many of the advantages of bigger setups at a reasonable price.**

dition to the spray gun, you will need a source of air, either a turbine (see pp. 31-34) or a compressor (see pp. 35-36). You'll also need air lines, hoses and various types of filters (see pp. 58-63).

Also, since spraying releases a fine cloud or mist of finish into the air, proper ventilation is more important than it would be if oil or varnish were being applied with a brush or rag. Removing the buildup of harmful vapors will require some sort of exhaust system or spray booth, which can be expensive to install and usually requires a lot of floor space. Even if you limit yourself to spraying water-based products, you will still need some type of fan to create enough air movement to keep the work environment clean and safe. Ventilation is discussed in detail on pp. 46-48.

Don't let the cost deter you from setting up your own spray system. Most manufacturers of industrial-quality spray equipment have introduced smaller, less expensive lines that are ideal for serious hobbyists and small professional shops. If you don't have the space or can't afford to set up a spray booth, you can consider using water-based products exclusively. Because they are nonflammable, you won't need to invest in expensive explosion-proof fans and fixtures. Good ventilation and a high-quality respirator should suffice.

Because spraying is a quick operation you will be able to reduce significantly the time and effort spent finishing even the smallest items. There is no doubt in my mind that the lower labor costs, combined with the professional, high-quality finishes I am consistently able to achieve, more than offset the initial expense and time required to set up a spray system. I know that my shop would not be able to survive without it.

# CHAPTER 2

# Choosing a System

The most important, and perhaps most confusing, decision you will make once you've decided to set up for spray finishing is what equipment to buy. In general, all spray systems do the same thing: They break up finish into tiny drops (a process called atomization) and deposit the drops onto the workpiece. Some systems break up the drops more finely than others, some move material at a faster rate, some are more efficient at placing material on the piece being finished and some work better with certain types of finishes than others. As a result, the type of system you should choose depends on what, how much and how fast you plan on spraying.

Every setup has three essential components: a gun, which sprays the finish; a cup or pot, which holds the finish; and a power system, which moves the finish material through the gun and atomizes it at the tip or air cap. Although there are several varieties and types of spray guns available, the insides of most spray guns are basically the same (see the drawing on p. 12). They contain inlets for air and fluid, fluid needles and tips and an air cap. The air line from the compressor or turbine attaches to the handle of the gun. Fluid enters the gun near the front, either from a cup mounted directly to the gun or from a remote pressure pot. The amount of fluid passing through the tip is adjusted by a screw on the back of the gun. Likewise, the amount of

**The system you should get will depend on where, what and how often you plan to spray. Choices include a compressed-air spray gun (above left), a portable turbine-driven system (above) and a small airless paint sprayer (left).**

## Anatomy of a Typical Spray Gun

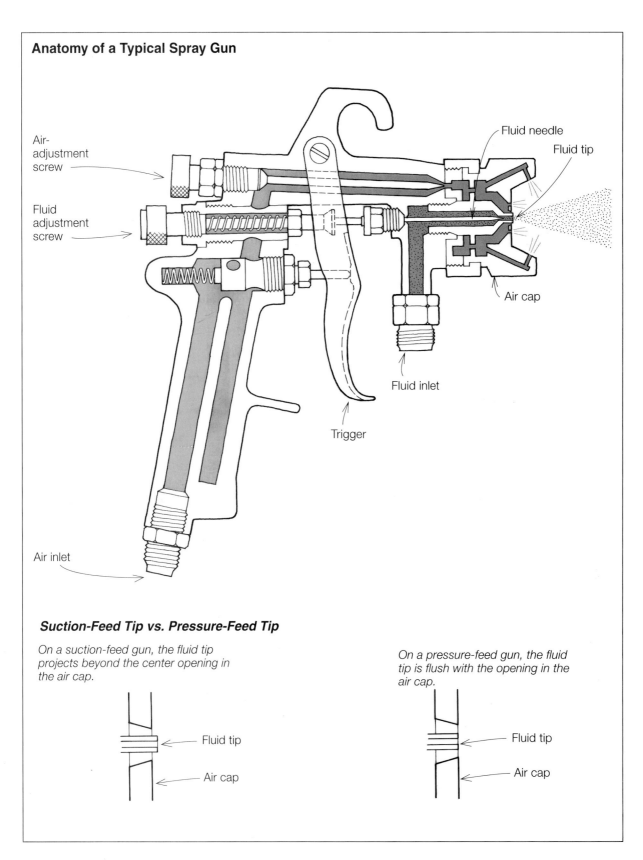

Air-adjustment screw

Fluid adjustment screw

Air inlet

Trigger

Fluid inlet

Fluid needle

Fluid tip

Air cap

### *Suction-Feed Tip vs. Pressure-Feed Tip*

*On a suction-feed gun, the fluid tip projects beyond the center opening in the air cap.*

Fluid tip

Air cap

*On a pressure-feed gun, the fluid tip is flush with the opening in the air cap.*

Fluid tip

Air cap

air passing through the air cap is controlled by another screw (air-adjustment screw or spreader valve) located above the first. Adjusting the two screws in unison allows you to control the rate of application.

A spray system also must have a container for holding the finish. These containers, which can range from a 4-oz. cup on a touch-up gun to a 10-gal. pressure pot, can be located below, above or away from the gun. The location of the container will determine how the material is fed into the gun, while the type of air cap determines how and where fluid is atomized.

As for powering systems, there are several different types available and numerous manufacturers from which to choose. If you are just starting out, take a look at mail-order catalogs and advertisements in woodworking magazines; also check out your local paint and hardware stores. You can telephone the manufacturing companies to find out their distributors near you. Systems include conventional air spray, airless sprayers, air-assisted airless, electrostatic and HVLP (high-volume, low-pressure) systems. Knowing how each type of gun works and what it is best suited for will help you sidestep the pitfall of spending a lot of money on something that may not be the best choice for your needs.

## Conventional spray guns

Spray guns can be classified by how the finish material is fed through the tip (by suction, by gravity or by pressure). Guns may further be categorized by whether the air and finish material are mixed outside the air cap (external mix) or inside the air cap (internal mix); and by whether the flow of air through the tip is continuous (bleeder) or trigger controlled (nonbleed).

### Suction-feed guns

On a suction-feed gun, the material container, usually a 1-qt. cup, is located below the gun (see the photo at right). Compressed air enters the inlet on the handle and moves through the gun to create a vacuum at the air cap. The lid of the cup has one or more vent holes, which allow outside air to enter the cup. The difference in pressure between the air leaving the gun at the tip and the air entering the vent holes creates a siphon that draws material up the fluid tube and into the gun. The material is then drawn through the fluid tip, where it mixes with the air coming from the cap and is atomized.

**A suction-feed spray gun, like this small touch-up unit, uses airflow to siphon material up from the cup into the fluid tip.**

**Guns that have the material container attached to the handle are practical for small jobs that don't require a lot of spraying. However, they are a bit awkward for reaching into cramped spaces.**

There are several ways to identify a suction-feed gun quickly. Most obviously, the material container is located below the gun. Also, the lid to the container will have one or more vent holes. Finally, the fluid tip on a suction-feed gun extends just beyond the face of the air cap (see the detail drawing at bottom left on p. 12).

Because some of the air entering the gun is needed to draw material to the fluid tip, suction-feed guns are not as efficient at transferring material from the gun to the finish surface as the other types of guns. Guns running on compressed air create a lot of overspray (see the drawing on p. 30), so ventilating the spray area is important. Also, because the holes in the lid vents must remain open at all times, you must be careful about holding the gun. If you tip it too far sideways, finish material may leak out of the vents, creating a mess and possibly plugging up the holes. For this reason, suction-feed guns are less than ideal in tight quarters such as the inside of a drawer or a cabinet (see the photo above).

## Gravity-feed guns

Gravity-feed guns (see the photo below) are easily identifiable by the material cup, which is located on top of the gun. The force of gravity allows the finish to flow from the cup down into the gun, eliminating the need for a fluid tube. Like suction-feed guns, gravity-feed guns have a vent hole that allows air to pass through the top of the cup, ensuring a constant flow of material. Since no atomizing air is needed to move material from the cup to the fluid tip, gravity-feed systems are more efficient and require less incoming air than suction-feed systems. As a result, you can usually use a fluid tip that is a size smaller than you would with a suction-feed gun. Less air and a smaller tip combine to give you better control of how and where the material is sprayed, and they also reduce the amount of overspray as well. In addition, because the material flows down to the gun, you are able to use just about every drop in the cup.

Gravity-feed guns are a good alternative to suction-feed systems because they are lightweight and relatively efficient. Gravity-feed guns come with material containers that range in capacity from 4 oz. to 1 qt., which makes them very versatile. The smaller-size cups come in handy for spot repairs, detailed finishing or other applications that don't require a lot of material. Smaller material cups also work well in tight spots or in situations where you are shifting among several colors or types of finishes.

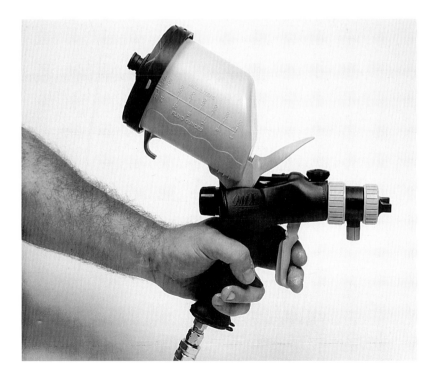

**A gravity-feed gun has the material container mounted on top of the handle. In this location it gives the gun better balance and takes some of the strain off the operator's wrist.**

## Pressure-feed systems

In a pressure-feed system (see the photos below), air is used to pressurize the material container, forcing fluid to the tip of the gun, where it is atomized by air passing through the air cap. Unlike suction-feed and gravity-feed systems, which have a hole in the material-cup lid, pressure-feed material containers must be sealed tightly in order to work properly. Any air leakage in the material container will result in a loss of fluid pressure, which may cause the gun to become starved for material.

Pressure-feed systems are easy to recognize. First, since there is no need to create any suction or siphoning action at the tip of the gun, the fluid tip is set flush with the air cap (see the detail drawing at bottom right on p. 12). Second, in a compressed-air pressure-feed system, the material container, or pressure pot, is usually located away from the gun. The container is pressurized, and material flows through a hose to the fluid intake on the gun. A separate hose entering the handle of the gun provides the air necessary for atomization.

Although most pressure-feed systems use remote material containers, there are exceptions. Some HVLP systems use incoming air to pressurize the cup, which is usually attached under the gun. A one-way check

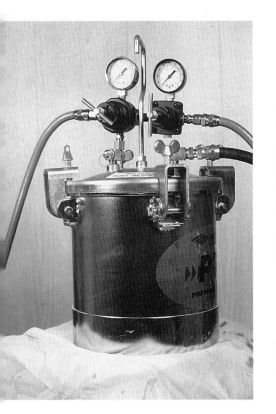

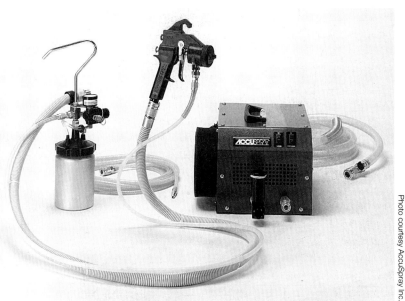

Photo courtesy AccuSpray Inc.

**Pressure-feed systems move material from a separate container through a fluid hose to the tip of the gun. They can run off a compressor, like the 2½-gal. pot on the left, or they can be part of a turbine-driven package, like the setup above.**

Recently, I was completing a project that used about 5 gal. of lacquer. There was a problem with one of the connections on the fluid hose leading from the pressure tank, so I had to spray the primer coat with a 1-qt. cup attached to the gun. The water-based lacquer was pigmented white, and the primer was extremely thick. Straining the lacquer, even after I had thinned the entire 5-gal. bucket, took

quite a while. Then I had to clean the strainer every time I refilled the cup. Once the cup was filled, it took about five minutes to empty it. I would then stop and fill the cup again, which added about 10 minutes of down time. If I moved quickly and had no other interruptions I could spray 1 qt. of material about every 15 minutes.

After fixing the connection on the fluid hose, I was able to use the 2½-gal. tank to apply the second coat of finish. It took about 10 minutes to strain the material into the pot and thin it. After that I was able to spray

the entire project without interruption in about an hour (compared with 2½ hours using the 1-qt. cup).

Obviously, if you plan on doing large amounts of spraying with the same material you would benefit from having a pressure-feed system. Even a pot as small as 2 qt. comes in handy on mid-sized jobs, since the number of times you have to refill the cup is cut in half.

---

valve (see the photo at right) allows air to move into the cup while preventing fluid from leaking into the air passages when the gun is tipped too far sideways or upside-down.

Because pressure-feed systems have valves that regulate air and fluid pressure (see the photo at left on the facing page), they offer several advantages over suction-feed and gravity-feed systems. First, because the air entering the pressure pot can be regulated, you have better control over the amount of positive pressure used to move fluid to the gun, so pressure-feed guns can spray finishes that would otherwise be too thick or heavy to be siphoned from a container. Second, the ability to control the atomizing air pressure allows you to adjust the pressure at the air cap. Higher pressure at the tip of the gun means that material can be atomized faster. As a result, the speed with which material is applied can be accelerated, so greater amounts of material can be sprayed in less time. This is especially useful if you have a lot of spraying to do or need to lay down multiple coats quickly.

Another advantage to pressure-feed systems is that the guns are light and easy to maneuver, especially in tight places. Because the fluid container is located away from the gun there is no bulky cup attached to the handle, just the fluid and air hoses. Taping the two hoses to-

A one-way check valve keeps finish material from leaking into the air passages when the gun is tipped too far sideways or upside-down.

**A few pieces of strategically placed duct tape keep the air and fluid hoses on a pressure-feed system from getting tangled.**

**A 2-qt. pressure cup comes in handy on jobs that are too small for a larger pressure pot.**

gether at a few points along their length (see the photo above left) makes them even easier to control and eliminates any chance that they will get tangled.

Perhaps the most important advantage offered by a pressure-feed system is the size of the material container. Pressure pots range from 2-qt. cups to 10-gal. (or larger) containers, which is enough material for several hours of spraying. The material can be thinned and strained into the pot, greatly reducing the need to interrupt production every time your 1-qt. cup runs dry (see the sidebar on p. 17). I have a 2½-gal. container that I use for larger production jobs. Filling the pot once versus the 10 times I would have to stop and fill a 1-qt. cup saves me a tremendous amount of aggravation.

Pressure-feed systems are ideal for someone who does a lot of spraying and are typically found in production shops. Unfortunately, they have a few drawbacks that make them impractical in certain situations. Pressure-feed systems take longer to clean than suction-feed or gravity-feed systems. Not only do you have to clean the gun, but you must also get all of the finish out of the fluid hose. Depending on the length of the line, this can be a time-consuming process. You must keep the pressure pot clean, too. Obviously, the bigger the container, the longer it takes to clean. I always use plastic pressure-pot liners (see the photo at right), which can be lifted out of the pressure pot, cleaned quickly and reused. If you are careful about how you pour the finish into the liner and don't move the pressure pot around much when it is full, you shouldn't have to clean the tank at all. Usually a quick wipe with a solvent-dampened rag will be all it needs.

Another disadvantage to pressure-feed systems is that they need a source of air to pressurize the tank. If you are already using a large compressor to run your spray system, this is not a problem. However, if you have a turbine-driven HVLP gun (see pp. 31-34) and you wish to use a pressure pot, you will need a separate air source. Many manufacturers offer pressure-tank systems that come mounted on carts (see the photo below). These self-contained units have their own air source mounted on the cart and work like any other pressure-feed system, although you still need the turbine to provide atomizing air to the gun. If you already have a turbine-driven HVLP gun and wish to increase the capacity of your system, a portable setup would be a good way to go.

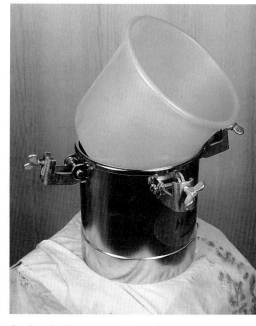

**A plastic liner simplifies the cleanup of a pressure pot. Compared to the cost of solvent, liners are inexpensive and can be reused many times.**

Photo courtesy AccuSpray Inc.

**A portable turbine with a large pressure pot is the system of choice for many professional painters who want the benefits of HVLP equipment and need to be able to spray large amounts of material in various locations.**

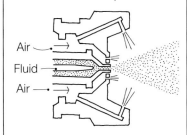
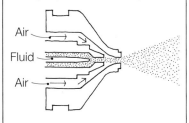
## External-mix vs. internal-mix guns

Spray guns are classified not only according to how the material gets to the fluid tip, but also by how the atomizing air mixes with the fluid at the air cap. In an external-mix gun (see the drawing at left), air and fluid are mixed outside the air cap. Guns of this type are extremely versatile and can be used to spray almost any material. They are ideal for spraying fast-drying finishes and lay down a high-quality coat of finely atomized material. Most of the guns on the market today use an external-mix air cap.

An internal-mix gun (see the drawing at left) combines the fluid and atomizing air inside the air cap. The atomized finish is then forced out of the air cap to the surface being finished. Internal-mix guns do not require the air volume and pressure associated with external-mix guns, so they are able to operate with less overspray. This need for less air pressure makes them better suited to situations where a good air supply is not readily available. Usually, you would find an internal-mix gun being used with small, portable compressors where a fine, furniture-quality finish is not necessary.

Internal-mix guns do not work well with fast-drying finishes. Because the fluid is atomized inside the air cap, it starts to dry before it leaves the tip of the gun. The tip of the gun will tend to clog, resulting in a poorer-quality finish. Because most of the finishes sprayed today are fast drying, occasions to use an internal-mix gun are limited. In fact, the only time I would recommend an internal-mix gun would be if your air source is insufficient or you plan only to spray slow-drying paint on the outside of a house or on projects that don't require a fine finish. Otherwise, stick with external-mix guns. Their ability to handle most types of material makes them a much better value.

## Bleeder vs. nonbleed guns

When choosing a type of spray gun, there is one final question to consider. Do you want a gun that has a constant stream of air passing through the tip, called a "bleeder"? Or do you want a "nonbleed" gun that shuts off the air flow when the trigger is released?

With both types of guns, the air flow through the cap precedes the flow of material. In the case of bleeder guns, air is always present before fluid is released. Nonbleed guns have a valve in the trigger that allows the flow of air to start a fraction of a second before any finish material is released. Regardless of the type of gun, air moving through the cap eliminates the chance that a stream of fluid could escape the gun before it is properly atomized. Also, the air passing through the gun can be used to remove any dust or large particles that may have settled on the surface to be finished before any fluid is released.

***Bleeder guns*** The discharge of air from the tip of a bleeder gun is constant. Depressing the trigger of the gun allows fluid to flow into that stream of air, where it is atomized. Bleeder guns offer a few advantages over nonbleed guns. Bleeder guns do not need any special mechanisms in the trigger or handle to allow the flow of air to be stopped. Because these guns have fewer working parts and are simpler in design, they are less expensive than nonbleed guns.

Because the flow of air through a bleeder gun is constant, there is no buildup of pressure in the air hose or lines. This is a real advantage when you are using a turbine-driven HVLP system. If the flow of air moving from the turbine through the gun is stopped and no other outlet is provided, excessive heat will build up in the turbine and burn out the motor.

Bleeder guns have a few disadvantages, especially if you are using compressed air to power the system. Since air loss through the gun is continuous, your compressor will have to work harder to deliver the right amount of air. With a bleeder gun you must also be careful where you point the tip when not actually spraying. The stream of air from the tip of the gun may kick up little clouds of dust if it is inadvertently allowed to come too close to the floor or wall, and a blast of air pointed directly at a freshly finished surface may cause the material to "crawl."

***Nonbleed guns*** A nonbleed gun has a valve mechanism in the handle that interrupts the flow of air to the tip of the gun when the trigger is released (see the photo below). These triggers have two stages. A

**The spring-loaded valve in the trigger mechanism of nonbleed guns controls the flow of air through the tip. This extra hardware makes nonbleed guns more expensive than bleeder guns.**

**A pressure-relief valve on the air hose prevents air buildup when used with a nonbleed gun. The large nut on the top of the valve controls how much air is released.**

slight pull opens the valve and allows air to move through the gun to the air cap. Depressing the trigger further begins the flow of material to the fluid tip.

Because there is no unnecessary air loss with nonbleed guns, they are a good choice for compressed-air systems. I also use a nonbleed gun with my turbine-driven HVLP setup. A pressure-relief valve located on the air hose opens automatically whenever air is not passing through the gun. By allowing a constant flow of air through the system, the valve (see the photo above) prevents heat from damaging the turbine.

It is said that nonbleed guns should not be used with turbine-driven systems because the relief valves do not allow enough air to escape from the turbine, and the resulting buildup of hot air will eventually burn out the motor. After more than two years of putting the same turbine and valve through a lot of heavy use, I have not noticed any problems with it or any decrease in its performance. I keep the valve open as far as it will go and always make sure it is clean and functioning properly. The valve and the air coming from it get very hot, so it is important to exercise caution in how you handle the valve and where you point it.

Nonbleed guns usually cost more than bleeders, which is a slight disadvantage. The extra parts in the trigger increase the complexity of the gun and lead to higher manufacturing costs. If you use a turbine, you also have the additional cost of the relief valve.

Given the choice, I prefer nonbleed guns because I can control how, when and where air is released from the gun. There is very little chance of accidentally misdirecting the air and ruining a finish.

# Air sources for conventional systems

When selecting a spray system you must decide not only on the type of gun to use, but also on how the gun will be powered. There are several different ways material can be atomized. Conventional compressed-air systems, airless sprayers, air-assisted airless and electrostatic systems are available. Some of these are better suited to certain applications than others and may not be appropriate in all situations. Understanding the options available, how they work and what they do best will help you set up the best system for your needs.

### Compressed air

Compressed-air spray guns were developed in the late 1800s and began to see heavy industrial use after the turn of the century. The automotive industry in particular was instrumental in developing spray technology. As auto makers searched for better and faster ways to integrate the painting process into their rapidly expanding assembly lines, spray systems were developed and improved, gradually evolving into the systems still in use today.

The popular idea of a spray gun is the conventional system powered by compressed air. The gun is hooked directly to a large air compressor, and material is atomized at relatively high pressures. The amount of air used to atomize the finish is limited only by the delivery capabilities of the compressor, and usually ranges from 30 psi to 90 psi.

The high pressure used with a conventional compressed-air gun offers an advantage over other systems. High air pressure creates extremely fine atomization. The material comes out of the gun at high velocity and can be applied quickly, which is ideal for applications where speed is essential.

Although the high pressure associated with compressed-air guns allows for fine atomization and rapid rates of application, it causes several problems that make this system less than ideal. The air entering the gun is highly compressed and expands rapidly once it leaves the tip of the gun, creating a fair amount of turbulence at the air cap, which causes a large amount of overspray. The velocity and pressure of the air atomize the finish material into a large cloud of mist that is hard to control.

Because the air leaves the gun at a high velocity, the finish material is deposited very fast. This leads to a problem known as "bounce back" (see the drawing on p. 30), where the finish bounces off the surface and comes back toward the gun or operator. The excessive overspray and bounce back caused by a compressed-air gun causes several problems. Because so much material is lost to overspray and bounce back, the transfer efficiency of compressed-air guns is fairly low. On average, you can hope to have 20% to 35% of your finish stay on the surface of your project, with the remainder being lost to overspray. When compared to the almost 100% transfer rate of a brush or rag, a compressed-air system does not seem to be very efficient, and you must plan on using a lot more finish material than you would when using a brush or rag.

The amount of overspray associated with a compressed-air system means you will need an extremely well-ventilated spray area or may have to install a spray booth. If only 35% of the finish material is being placed on the workpiece, where is the remainder going? Everywhere. Compressed-air systems create a cloud of overspray that will rapidly permeate the surrounding air (see the sidebar on the facing page). If the room is not ventilated properly, the overspray will fill the entire area and eventually settle over everything. This cloud of mist is not only a health hazard that makes wearing a respirator essential, but could, depending on the material being sprayed, also create the potential for an explosion or fire.

In spite of their drawbacks, compressed-air systems are still widely used, especially in production shops and the automotive business. Their ability to atomize all types of finish materials, combined with their high rate of application, makes them ideal for certain situations. However, low transfer efficiency combined with the need for adequate air movement and an air compressor make them relatively expensive to operate. In fact, in some parts of the country, they do not meet strict environmental regulations and can no longer be used.

I'll never forget the first time I used a conventional compressed-air gun to spray finish. I was working in my garage shop and had full-size sheets of plywood that needed to be finished in a hurry. Brushing on the solvent-based varnish would have taken too long and would have resulted in a less than acceptable finish. Fortunately, or so I thought, someone had given me a cheap compressed-air gun. I hooked it up to my portable compressor and began blasting away.

At first I was thrilled. The material was atomizing nicely and flowing onto the surface of the wood so fast I couldn't believe it. In a matter of minutes I had one panel completely coated and was on to the next one. It was winter, so I could not open the overhead garage door for ventilation. I wasn't too concerned about this though; after all, I had only six sheets of plywood to finish, and the first one went so quickly that I would be done in no time. I had a small fan blowing out of the side door, so airing out the room certainly wasn't going to be a problem.

About halfway through the second panel I began to notice something strange—I could not see what I was doing. Must be the light, I figured. Shifting positions to get a better view, I hurriedly continued spraying. This worked fine for another 30 seconds or so before, once again, I couldn't see what I was doing.

Frustrated, I put down the gun and stepped back to assess the situation. As I was looking around for a place with better lighting, I noticed that the entire garage was filled with what appeared to be smoke. Quickly I checked the shop for fire and then looked outside to be sure everything was okay. When I stepped back into the building from the crisp, clear winter air, I couldn't believe my eyes. The entire shop was filled with a cloud of smelly overspray.

Believing there must be something wrong with the gun, I cleaned it and fiddled with the settings and adjustments for the next hour. Eventually I came to the conclusion that the gun was working fine, and I would have to continue as before. Needless to say, I finished the last four sheets of plywood as fast as I could, cleaned the gun, and my glasses, and left the shop.

When I returned a few hours later the air had cleared, though the smell still lingered, and I had six beautifully finished panels. I also had a layer of varnish over everything else in the shop. I spent the rest of the day cleaning the overspray off my tools and equipment, and I swore I would never use a compressed-air gun again without adequate ventilation.

## Airless

As the name implies, airless sprayers do not use any air to move material through the gun. Instead of a compressor or turbine, airless sprayers use a pump to propel the finish material through a small tip. The pressure required to move the fluid through the tip is usually very high, ranging from 1,200 psi to 3,000 psi.

Because liquid is forced through the tip of an airless sprayer at high pressures, large amounts of material can be delivered very quickly. Airless sprayers can handle the greatest variety of finishes, including heavy-bodied latex and oil paints, and they offer better transfer efficiency rates than conventional air-spray systems. Because fluid is moved to the gun by a pump, no special containers are needed to hold the paint. In fact, the fluid intake tube can usually be stuck right inside the can of finish (see the photo below). This direct arrangement speeds production and reduces the amount of time spent on cleanup.

Most of the professional painters I know use airless sprayers at one time or another. Because the systems are usually portable (see the photo on the facing page), they are easy to move from one job to the next. Their ability to spray large quantities of most materials makes

**Because airless sprayers operate at high pressure, they are able to move a lot of material in a hurry. This makes them ideal for painting large surfaces, like the side of a house.**

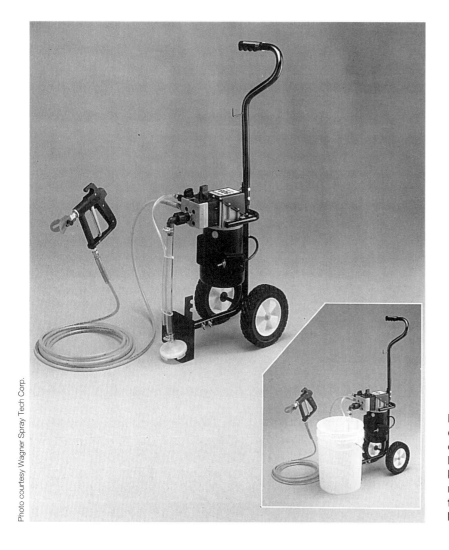

Photo courtesy Wagner Spray Tech Corp.

**Professional painters probably own a portable airless sprayer capable of handling 5-gal. buckets of paint. If you only have one house to paint, it may pay to rent a unit like this from your local paint or hardware store.**

them ideal for production situations, such as painting houses or large decks. Renting an airless sprayer from a paint store is a good option if you have to do a lot of painting on one particular project.

Unfortunately, the speed and versatility of airless sprayers come at the expense of quality. Because the material is pumped through the tip at great pressure, there is no atomizing air to break it up into finer particles. As a result, the finishes obtained with airless sprayers are often less than desirable. Therefore airless sprayers are a poor choice for furniture finishing, where a smoother, more finely atomized finish is usually required.

### Air-assisted airless

Air-assisted airless systems combine the best of airless systems with conventional spray guns. Like airless systems, they use a pump to move great quantities of material through the gun quickly, while simultaneously introducing air at the tip of the gun to create an atomized finish. The fluid pressure, though not as high as with airless systems, ranges from 600 psi to 1,000 psi, while the air pressure necessary to atomize the material usually falls between 15 psi and 30 psi. Because air-assisted airless systems use less air pressure than conventional spray guns, their transfer efficiency rates are higher, from 40% to 65%.

Air-assisted airless sprayers are relatively new systems that are generally found in production situations. Their ability to atomize a variety of materials, combined with high-speed application, makes them ideal for the stationary finishing lines found in larger furniture shops.

### Electrostatic

Electrostatic spray systems depend on electrical charges to draw finish from the gun to the surface being sprayed. As the material leaves the tip of the gun it is given an electrical charge. The particles of fluid are then drawn to the surface of the object, which carries an opposing electrical charge. Transfer efficiencies are high (55% to 95%) and result in even coats of uniform thickness over the entire piece. Therefore electrostatic finishing is ideal for round, unusually shaped or hard-to-spray pieces. Systems like this are usually found only in large production settings and are too costly and impractical for the casual user. However, as air quality becomes of greater concern, regulations concerning transfer efficiencies of spray equipment are becoming stricter. As a result, the need for manufacturers to develop and improve spray systems may someday make electrostatic finishing more affordable and practical for smaller shops.

# HVLP systems

There has been a great deal of publicity in recent years about high-volume, low-pressure systems, a new technology that is revolutionizing the spray-finishing industry. Conflicting information and exaggerated advertising claims have created a lot of confusion about the way in which HVLP spraying works. As a result, HVLP spraying may seem mysterious and complex, when in fact it is a simple system that borrows and improves upon many characteristics of conventional spraying with compressed air.

HVLP spray systems were developed in France in the 1950s in an effort to save finishing material by increasing transfer efficiency. They were introduced to America on a commercial basis in the early 1980s, but didn't really catch on. Although HVLP systems offered higher transfer-efficiency rates than conventional spray systems, most finishers were reluctant to switch to a new and unproven technology.

However, not long after HVLP guns were introduced, California's South Coast Air Quality Management District (SCAQMD) mandated that all spray equipment comply with strict new regulations. Since then, interest in HVLP spraying has grown, as have the number of manufacturers and types of systems being offered. The competition among manufacturers has led to an improvement in HVLP technology and has also brought down the price of good-quality systems to an affordable level.

## How HVLP works

Since HVLP spraying evolved from compressed-air technology, there are many similarities between the two systems. They both operate under the same principle—mixing a stream a fluid with an air source to create atomization—and the guns generally look the same. What separates HVLP spraying from conventional compressed-air systems is the volume and pressure of the air moving through the spray gun and how efficiently that air atomizes the fluid.

Compressed-air systems use a moderate volume of air at relatively high pressures to move the fluid through the gun. In contrast, HVLP systems must, by definition, operate at 10 psi or less at the air cap. To make up for this lower air pressure, HVLP guns use more air moving at a slower speed. The greater volume of air passing through the gun compensates for the loss of speed, or pressure, to atomize the fluid properly. The result is a softer, more controllable spray pattern that puts more of the finish where it is supposed to be. The problems of

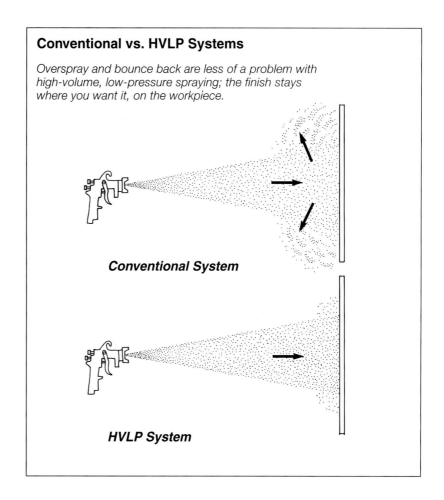

**Conventional vs. HVLP Systems**

*Overspray and bounce back are less of a problem with high-volume, low-pressure spraying; the finish stays where you want it, on the workpiece.*

**Conventional System**

**HVLP System**

excessive overspray and bounce back associated with compressed-air guns are greatly reduced (see the drawing above). Accordingly, the transfer-efficiency ratios for HVLP spraying are much greater, from 65% to 90%. (In fact, to comply with the regulations that define HVLP spraying, transfer efficiency must be at least 65%.) The chart on the facing page compares transfer efficiencies of commonly available systems. Greater transfer efficiency means you need less material to finish a project. When compared with compressed-air spraying, HVLP systems will require only one-quarter to one-half as much material to cover the same piece.

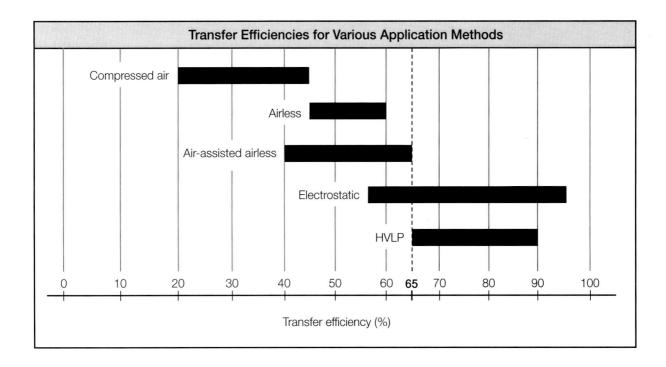

**Transfer Efficiencies for Various Application Methods**

Transfer efficiency (%)

# Air sources for HVLP systems

There are two kinds of HVLP systems: those that are driven by a turbine and those that run on compressed air. The method you choose will depend on the types of material you plan to spray, how much room you have in your shop and how much money you can spend.

### Turbines

For the small-shop owner, turbine-driven HVLP spray guns are probably the best thing that has happened to spray finishing. The entire system can be purchased in one neat package—complete with a gun, turbine and air hose—for about the same amount of money as a decent drill press or table saw.

A turbine is an industrial-strength vacuum-cleaner motor that generates a high volume of slowly moving air. Turbines come in several sizes and are suited for different tasks. Being sure you have the right size turbine is the first step toward successful HVLP spraying, since an undersized unit will lead to less than ideal results.

Turbines are rated according to the number of fans that are mounted to the motor, with each fan representing one "stage." The more stages a turbine has, the more pressure it is capable of generating. Fan diameters can be either 5.7 in. or 7.2 in., the larger of which produces a greater volume of air flow.

All turbines essentially do the same thing: they draw air in through a filter, move it through the fan stages or compression chambers and discharge it to the air outlet. How a turbine moves this air depends on the type of motor housed in its sheet-metal or plastic box.

***Bypass vs. thru-flow turbines***  Most of today's turbines use bypass motors that have separate intake and cooling fans. Bypass turbines have chambers to keep the incoming air separate from the cooling air, thereby eliminating the chance of unfiltered air entering the system through the exhaust vents on the side of the unit. If for some reason the air outlet of a bypass turbine became plugged, the separate cooling fan would reduce the risk of heat buildup inside the unit and help prevent the motor from burning out.

Thru-flow turbines, which are usually single- or double-stage units, draw air in one side of the motor, then pass it through the fans and out the other side. The same fan that draws air into the unit is used to cool the air. If the air outlet on a thru-flow turbine is blocked off, warm air building up inside the motor would burn it out very quickly. If you ever come across a thru-flow turbine, chances are it will be a small, inexpensive unit.

***Peripheral vs. tangential systems***  Turbines may also be classified as peripheral or tangential, depending on how the incoming air is discharged from the motor to the air hose. In a peripheral system, air enters through the bottom of the motor, moves through the stages and is discharged in a 360° ring around the middle of the motor. An exhaust collar placed around the motor gathers the escaping air and channels it to the hose outlet. Peripheral discharge is a relatively inefficient way to move air to the hose, and, like thru-flow systems, it is usually found on small, inexpensive models.

A tangential turbine draws air through the fan stages and directs it to the air outlet through a 2-in. dia. "horn" located on the side of the motor. Tangential turbines are much better at moving air directly to the air hose than peripheral systems, and are good-quality turbines. In fact, most of today's turbines are bypass, tangential units.

***Selecting the turbine that's right for you***  The key to successful turbine-driven HVLP spraying lies in whether or not the turbine is capable of delivering enough pressure to atomize the material you plan on spraying. Turbines are rated by how many psi they can deliver. However, manufacturers often use different methods of rating their turbines, which may be confusing and misleading.

What's important to consider is how much air pressure the turbine can deliver to the tip of the gun, or air cap, where atomization takes place. Although a two-stage turbine may work well for lighter-bodied materials, at best it will deliver around 4 psi at the tip of the gun. This is simply not enough pressure to atomize some heavy-bodied or high-solid materials. In order to take full advantage of your HVLP system, you should consider a turbine with at least three stages. Most three-stage units are capable of delivering 5 psi to 6 psi to the tip of the gun, which will allow you to atomize a greater variety of finishes.

I have a three-stage unit that works well with most varnishes, lacquers and water-based products, although I have to thin heavier materials such as pigmented lacquer primers or latex paint in order to get good atomization. For the average small shop or casual finisher, a three-stage unit is big enough to handle the most common applications and

| TURBINE-DRIVEN SYSTEMS AT A GLANCE | |
|---|---|
| Advantages | Disadvantages |
| **Portability.** Because the turbines are compact and lightweight, the entire system is portable. This is useful if you do any job-site work such as painting or touch-up. Also, you can move the unit around your shop, which makes it easier to spray large objects that may not fit in your spray room or booth. | **Pressure-generating limitations.** The air flow and pressure generated by a turbine can be reduced by settings on the turbine or air hose, but they cannot be increased beyond the maximum limit of the unit. Many turbines simply do not generate enough air pressure to atomize all materials properly. If you plan on spraying a lot of heavy-bodied finishes, you may have to thin the coatings or buy a larger, more expensive turbine. |
| **Low maintenance.** Turbines require little maintenance. If you keep your unit away from large amounts of dust and overspray, your maintenance will be limited to an occasional filter cleaning. | **Noise.** Turbines are loud. The turbine sounds like a large vacuum-cleaner motor, which, when running for a long time, can become annoying. Hearing protection becomes a necessity when using turbines to spray. |
| **Minimal space and equipment.** Turbines do not require the space and air lines that a compressed-air system must have. All you need is an air hose, a gun and an electrical outlet, and you are ready to spray. | **Need to switch on and off repeatedly.** The turbine must be switched on every time you start to spray and then turned off when you are done. This may seem like a minor nuisance, but if your turbine is located outside your spray area, and you don't have it hooked into a conveniently located wall switch, you will spend a lot of time walking back and forth from the turbine to the gun. |
| **Affordability.** Most HVLP turbine-driven units come as complete packages and are affordable for even the smallest shop. Good systems can be purchased for about the same cost as a decent stationary power tool. | |

**The air hose on the left is fairly heavy and stiff. It can get tiring to lug around all day. The hose on the right is much lighter and supple, but it is liable to develop splits and cracks and will fall apart more quickly, especially if you step on it.**

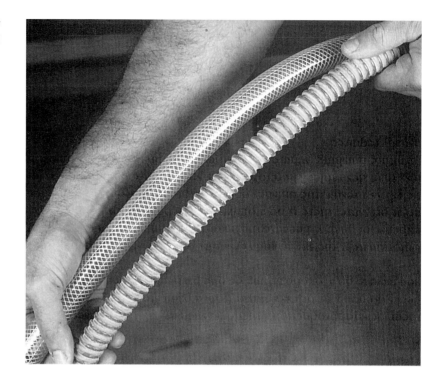

is probably the best value for the money. However, if you spray a lot of heavy-bodied materials or need to set up for production, you should look to larger units. Currently available five- and seven-stage turbines can not only atomize most materials but also run more than one gun at a time.

Whatever turbine you select, setting it up and using it couldn't be easier. Simply attach the air hose (and relief valve if you are using a non-bleed gun) to the air outlet, plug it in and turn it on. The only thing you need to worry about is where you place your turbine. Since a turbine needs a large amount of cool, clean air to function properly, it should be located as far away from the spray area as possible. Ideally, you should set your turbine outside of your spray booth or in another room. This will help prevent overspray from being drawn into the intake filter, clogging it and shortening the life of the filter and motor. (For more on turbine placement see pp. 50-51.)

A common complaint with turbine-driven HVLP systems is that the air hose is too heavy or bulky. That depends, of course, on the type of hose you use (see the photo above). Hoses that are made of lightweight plastic with a reinforcing wire running through them are not only relatively inexpensive, but also light and easy to handle. Hoses made of heavy-duty plastic or rubber are bulkier and stiffer, but will withstand a lot more abuse.

## Compressed air

When HVLP systems were first developed, they depended primarily on turbines as their air source. However, compressed-air and conversion HVLP guns have been available for several years and are starting to have an impact on the market. By combining the benefits of HVLP spraying with the versatility of compressed air, compressed-air and conversion HVLP setups offer the best of both worlds.

In a compressed-air HVLP system, air pressure entering the gun may be as high as 80 psi. It is converted to low pressure inside the gun, either through the design of the air chambers or at a special baffle located at the tip of the gun. In order to achieve true HVLP spraying, the air used to pressurize the material container must also be regulated. This may be done by the air-intake valve on a remote pressure tank or, if the material container is attached to the gun, by a separate regulator mounted on the handle of the gun.

With a conversion system, the air pressure must be reduced to 10 psi or less before it reaches the gun. This is usually accomplished by a regulator mounted on the wall between the filters and the air hose.

HVLP guns that are powered by compressed air have many advantages over turbine-driven systems. With a compressed-air system you have better control over both the atomizing air and the fluid pressure. Also, a properly sized compressor should be capable of generating higher pressure at the air cap than most turbines, which is useful if you are spraying high-solids finishes that are difficult to atomize. The ability to control air and fluid pressure through a compressed-air system allows you to spray heavier materials with less thinning.

Speed is another advantage of using compressed air to run your gun. Because you have control over the air pressure, you can increase the rate at which material is atomized. If you do a lot of spraying you will appreciate this feature since it helps greatly reduce the time needed to coat an object.

Although conversion and compressed-air HVLP guns are an attractive alternative to turbine-driven systems, they have a few drawbacks. They require a relatively high volume of air (anywhere from 10 to 20 cubic feet per minute, or cfm) at pressures ranging from 50 psi to 80 psi. In order to achieve this kind of air delivery, you must have a compressor of at least 3 hp, but 5 hp would be better. You also need proper air lines, filters and regulators. If you already have a compressed-air system in your shop, the cost of a spray gun will not be much. However, the initial expense of setting up an entire system from scratch will be considerable.

Another disadvantage of using a compressed-air HVLP system is that with a standard system you lose the portability offered by a turbine. The size and electrical requirements of the compressor, combined with fixed air lines and filters, obviously limit the mobility of the system. Large compressed-air systems are suitable only for stationary set-ups where all the spraying is done in one location.

***Portable compressed-air HVLP systems***  Most HVLP guns that run on compressed air require large compressors that must be fixed in place. However, that does not mean that compressed-air HVLP guns cannot be used outside the shop. In fact, many manufacturers are offering new guns that run off compressors as small as 1.5 hp. These guns vary from little touch-up models with 8-oz. cups to larger units with compressors and 2-gal. pressure pots mounted on portable carts. The smaller units are ideal for spot repairs and quick refinishing jobs, while the bigger units can move from room to room as you finish the interior of an entire house.

All these portable units offer the same advantages of compressed-air HVLP spraying, including a soft spray, high transfer efficiency and adjustable air pressure ranging from 1 psi to 10 psi. You may have to thin the material a little more, and the compressor will work harder, but otherwise these systems operate the same as any compressed-air HVLP system.

Because these guns create such a small amount of overspray, they are ideal for use in the home or on job sites. Recently I had to do some repair work on some built-in cabinets in a new home. The walls were painted, the floors were freshly finished and the people had begun moving in their furniture. Because the small touch-up gun I was using is accurate and easy to control, I needed only to protect the surrounding area with some tape on the wall next to the cabinets and a drop cloth on the floor. Rather than trying to make spot repairs, I ended up recoating the surfaces of all four cabinets. The whole job, even with a small gun and 1.5-hp compressor, took less than a half-hour. Once refinished, the cabinets looked great, and there was no evidence of overspray anywhere in the room. In fact, if it hadn't been for the smell of the lacquer, no one would ever have known I had been there.

## H*VLP spraying: myth vs. fact*

Because HVLP spray guns are relatively new, there's a lot of confusion about how the system works. Following is a comparison of myths and facts to illustrate the way the system actually operates.

### Efficiency
*Myth:* HVLP spraying is almost as efficient as using a brush, with transfer rates that approach 100%.

*Fact:* It is true that HVLP spray guns are extremely efficient, especially when compared to conventional compressed-air spraying. Although transfer efficiencies can be as high as 90% under ideal conditions, they are more typically 65% to 70%. And although this is a great improvement over the 20% to 45% transfer rate of compressed-air guns, it is still far short of the nearly 100% rate for a brush or rag.

### Size
*Myth:* The size of turbine you use depends on how often and how much material you spray.

*Fact:* The size of the turbine depends on the *type* of material you spray, not on how much. Smaller turbines cannot generate enough pressure at the tip of the gun to atomize thick or high-viscosity materials such as latex paint.

### Speed
*Myth:* HVLP guns are slower than compressed-air systems.

*Fact:* It is true that turbine-driven systems do not lay down material as fast as compressed-air systems. However, if a compressed-air or conversion-HVLP system is sized properly, it will lay down material just as quickly as a conventional gun. Insufficient rates of application are usually caused by a failure to get enough air and fluid to the gun, not by the gun itself. An undersized turbine or compressor, air lines that are too small or leak and dirty or clogged fluid passages can combine to slow down production rates unnecessarily.

### Heat
*Myth:* The warm, dry air generated by turbines helps the finish flow out better and dry faster.

*Fact:* Certainly it is true that it is better to spray with warm, dry air than with cold, damp air. Moisture in the air can ruin a finish, which is why compressed air must be filtered. However, the warm air generated by a turbine does not help the finish flow out better or dry faster. In fact, it may actually be detrimental to some finishes by causing solvents that are necessary for proper flow and drying to "flash off" at the tip of the gun before they have a chance to make it to the finish surface.

The only way heat can help a finish is if the finish itself is heated before it is sprayed. For this purpose special material heaters can be used, and the pre-warmed finish will flow out better and dry more quickly.

### Guns
*Myth:* All HVLP guns that run on compressed air are "conversion" guns.

*Fact:* There are actually two types of HVLP guns that get their power from compressed air. Conversion guns have a regulator mounted somewhere between the gun and the compressor that lowers the atomizing air pressure before it gets to the gun. Compressed-air HVLP guns allow air under high pressure to enter the gun (usually from 50 psi to 80 psi) and be converted to low pressure either through a series of valves and chambers or by a specially designed baffle located near the tip of the gun.

# CHAPTER 3

# Setting Up a Spray System

Before you begin applying finish you'll need to set up your equipment in an area that is appropriate for spraying. Depending on the type of material you plan to spray and the quality of finish you hope to achieve, your spray area may be as complex as an industrial-quality spray booth complete with an explosion-proof fan and vapor-tight light fixtures or as simple as a garage with a fan and an open door.

No matter what you plan on using as a spray area, you should check with your local building department before proceeding. If you spray water-based products on a limited basis in your garage or basement, the building codes may not be a problem. However, the requirements and restrictions concerning the use of solvent-based materials and spray booths are very specific and become even more complex for professional shops. The last thing you want is to spend a lot of money on spray equipment and then discover that the local fire codes won't allow you to use it the way you had planned.

## Spray booths

In a perfect world, anyone who wanted to spray finish materials would have access to an industrial spray booth. Spray booths make the process easier and more efficient by providing a well-lit, clean, safe environment that is free of dust or other foreign matter that might ruin a finish. Spray booths also help by employing a fan and filters that rapidly remove overspray from the surrounding air. This not only cre-

**Spray booths come in a variety of shapes and sizes. This small touch-up booth can sit on a workbench or table; it's ideal for spraying small objects where shop space is limited.**

ates a smoother finish but is healthier for the operator as well. Since all the booth is used for is spraying, no other operations take place there that could contaminate the area. If the booth is big enough, there is plenty of room to introduce supplemental lighting. Also, pieces can be left in the booth until they are dry to the touch, so you don't have to worry about spraying something and then having it sit in a room where someone may be running a table saw or sander.

There are two types of spray booths available, dry and wet-recovery systems. A dry system uses disposable paper or fiber filters to catch the overspray before it can be vented outside. This booth is most commonly found in the average small- to medium-size shop and is relatively inexpensive and readily available. A wet-recovery, or "waterwash" booth uses water to trap particles of finish. This type of booth is fairly sophisticated and generally found in large production shops where spraying is a constant activity. Because waterwash booths are designed for heavy use and would not be practical for the average hobbyist or small shop, I will not discuss them here.

The first decision you have to make is what size booth you need. Spray booths come in a number of sizes, from 3-ft. square touch-up booths to 20-ft. wide floor models. Obviously, the choice you make depends on what you plan to spray.

Photo courtesy Binks Manufacturing Co.

**Bench booths are larger than touch-up booths and come with a built-in workbench.**

## Touch-up booths

If you intend to use your spray booth to finish small objects (such as jewelry boxes or craft items), you will need only a small touch-up booth or bench-top model (see the photo on p. 39). A touch-up, or bench-top, booth is a small version of a walk-in floor booth. The working area is usually about 3 ft. square, and the booth can either sit on top of your own workbench or be attached to manufacturer-supplied legs. A touch-up booth is constructed from exactly the same materials and uses the same filters as a floor model, but it has a smaller motor and exhaust fan. These booths are ideal if you don't have the floor space for a larger booth.

## Bench booths

If you have a little more room and plan on spraying slightly larger objects, you may want to install a bench booth. Bench booths are a cross between small touch-up booths and large floor models. A bench booth sits on the floor and contains a built-in bench or working platform. Bench booths may require anywhere from 15 sq. ft. to 35 sq. ft. of floor space and about 7 ft. to 8 ft. of headroom. The overall size of the bench booth you choose depends not only on the size of the pieces being sprayed, but also on how much space you have.

Like touch-up booths, bench booths use the same components and filters as large models and have fans and exhaust stacks sized accordingly. The variety of sizes available make bench booths a good option for someone who doesn't have the floor space for a walk-in booth but still needs enough room for finishing larger objects such as shutters, balusters or component parts.

## Floor booths

If you are in the business of making high-end office furniture, you may need a booth large enough to handle a 10-ft. conference table. In that case, you will need a floor model or walk-in booth. These large booths come in a staggering array of sizes and configurations. The number of sizes available should allow you to select a booth that fits both your spraying needs and your floor space.

A good way to determine what size booth you need is to take the average dimensions of the furniture you will be spraying and add 2 ft. to all sides. For example, the average cabinets I make in my shop are from 2 ft. to 4 ft. wide, about 2 ft. deep and maybe 3 ft. tall. Therefore I could use a booth with an inside working area of 6 ft. to 8 ft. wide, 6 ft. deep and 7 ft. tall.

However, before buying a booth this size, I considered the size of the area where I'd be placing the booth. A floor booth demands floor space slightly wider than its outside dimensions so there will be ac-

Photo courtesy DeVilbiss Spray Booth Products

**Walk-in floor models can accommodate large projects, but they take up a lot of shop space.**

cess to the exhaust chamber and installation will be easier. The room where my booth was to go is 9 ft. wide, which meant an 8-ft. booth would just fit.

Headroom also played a role. My shop has 13-ft. high ceilings, so the booth could be as high as 12 ft. As I mentioned before, adding 2 ft. to the height of my cabinets meant I needed a booth 7 ft. tall. However, I also spray many unusually shaped objects that I like to hang from hooks, so I decided to add an extra foot to the height of my booth to give me a bit more overhead working area. In fact, if I'd had some extra money at the time, I would have bought a 10-ft. high booth.

Finally, I considered the depth of the area I had to work with. Again, according to the "2-ft." guide, a minimum of 6 ft. of working depth would be needed to finish a 2-ft. deep cabinet comfortably. When calculating how much room you need, keep in mind that spray booths have an exhaust chamber behind the working area that adds anywhere from 2½ ft. to 4 ft. to the overall depth of the booth. Therefore, a booth with 6 ft. of working depth may have an overall outside dimension of 8½ ft. to 10 ft.

In my shop, depth was not a problem so I was able to accommodate the 9 ft. 2 in. needed for my 6-ft. booth quite easily. In fact, since I had the space, I added 2-ft. extension panels to give me an increased working depth of 8 ft. I find the extra 2 ft. not only gives me more room to move, but also allows me to pull the objects being sprayed away from the filters, reducing the air flow enough that temperamental finishes such as water-based lacquers don't get pulled as easily toward the fan.

## Spray-booth accessories

Once you have determined how big a booth you need, you will have to decide which options to add, beginning with the type of motor for the fan. You'll also need good lighting, as well as properly sized filters for catching overspray.

*Fan motors*  If you plan on spraying only water-based, nonflammable materials, a regular motor should suffice. However, if you spray a lot of solvent-based materials you will need an explosion-proof motor. Before you purchase a spray booth you should check with your local fire inspector to determine what type of motor you will need to satisfy building codes. Even though I usually spray water-based materials, I made sure my booth came with an explosion-proof motor and spark-proof fan. Now I have the flexibility to use different materials if I need to, and I know that my booth will be in compliance if the local codes should happen to change.

You must also consider the electrical requirements of the motor before you buy a spray booth. Most industrial-quality spray booths come with a three-phase motor as standard equipment. If you don't have three-phase power in your shop, you will have to be sure to request a single-phase motor, which is usually offered as an option.

*Lighting*  If you purchase a touch-up or small bench booth, you will have to provide your own source of light. Overhead lights are offered as an option on some of the larger bench booths and come as standard equipment on most floor models. All industrial-quality floor booths should be equipped with at least one light fixture, and bigger models may come with as many as six. No matter how many lights you have in your booth, be sure they are "vapor tight," and are rated for use in hazardous locations. Again, be sure to check with your local building officials before purchasing your booth since they may require special explosion-proof fixtures that conform to a stricter rating.

As you add extension panels or increase the size of your booth, you may want to add more lights. Lights were not an option with the 2-ft. extension panels I added to my booth. However, if I had stepped up to a 3-ft. extension, I could have had an additional set of lights. If you can

**Extra lighting helps even if you have a well-lit spray booth. The bright halogen light on a portable stand shown here is useful when working with water-based finishes. When working with flammable materials, be sure all your lighting is explosion proof.**

afford the extra money for the lights, they would be worth it. If you want to increase the size of your booth and can't afford the extra lights, you can always introduce your own light sources for a fraction of the cost. In my own spray booth I have the room to move a free-standing light around as I am working and can position it where I need it for optimum visibility (see the photo above).

*Filters* There are several manufacturers of filter material, and, not surprisingly, each claims to have the best product. In fact, though, most industrial-quality filters will do a good job of capturing finish particles. The most important consideration is to use filters that are designed to fit in your type of booth. Using improperly fitted filters will increase the amount of cleaning you have to do and possibly shorten the life-span of your fan. Don't even think of using furnace filters—they are designed to catch relatively large particles of dust and simply are not capable of filtering finely atomized overspray.

**A manometer measures the static pressure inside a spray booth in terms of inches of water column. Mounted on the side of the booth, the manometer lets you know when your filters need changing.**

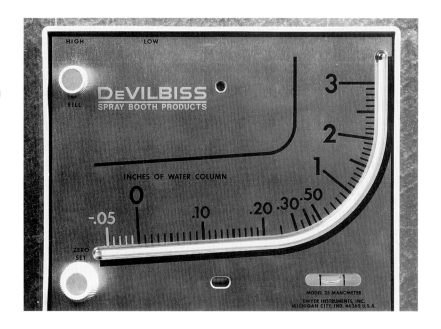

I inspect all of the filters in my booth both before and after spraying and change them as soon as it becomes necessary. I can tell when they need to be changed with the help of a manometer, or "draft gauge." This manometer (see the photo above), which came as standard equipment on my booth, is mounted on the outside wall near the filter area and measures the difference in air pressure between the two sides of the filter. The gauge indicates when the air passages are becoming restricted, thereby letting you know when the filters are loaded and need to be replaced.

If the booth you are thinking of buying does not have a manometer as standard equipment, you should give serious consideration to purchasing one as an option. Failure to keep your filters clean will adversely affect the efficiency of your spray booth in several ways. Clogged filters will lead to an unnecessary buildup of overspray on the fan blades, which may in turn put a heavy strain on the motor, shortening its working life. Also, by failing to remove particles of overspray efficiently, dirty filters create a dirty work area, which will lower the quality of your finishes. And failure to keep your booth clean by following a regular maintenance schedule may be a violation of local or federal codes, which could result in stiff penalties. But if your filters are designed to fit in your booth, and if you install them properly and change them on a regular basis, you should have no problems.

For more on keeping your spray booth clean, see the sidebar on the facing page.

## Keeping a spray booth clean

In addition to filters, there are several other products offered by various manufacturers that will help improve the performance of your booth. Keeping your booth clean is extremely important, and many of these products are designed to make the cleaning and maintenance process easier. I have found two products in particular to be helpful: peelable wall coatings and flame-retardant floor coverings. The wall coating (see the photo at top right) is simply a paintlike product that can be sprayed or rolled onto the walls of the booth. The product I use is water-based and does not present any hazardous storage or disposal problems. When the walls of my booth become excessively dirty with the buildup of overspray, I simply peel the coating off and throw it away. A new coat can be sprayed on in a matter of minutes and dries to the touch equally fast.

Keeping the floor of a spray booth clean can also be a chore since gravity tends to help overspray accumulate fairly quickly. I combat this problem with the help of a flame-retardant paper that can be rolled up and thrown away when it becomes covered with paint. This paper proves especially useful when spraying contact cement, which leaves a

Photo courtesy Chemco Manufacturing Co.

Photo courtesy Chemco Manufacturing Co.

**Above: Peelable wall coverings help keep a spray booth clean. When the amount of overspray on the walls of the booth becomes excessive, the coating can be peeled off to expose a clean surface.**

**Left: A white, flame-retardant covering rolled over the floor of a spray booth helps keep the booth clean and bright.**

thick, sticky mess on the floor. The paper (see the photo above) comes in rolls of various sizes and is available in different thicknesses and strengths.

Both the floor covering and peelable wall coating come in bright white, which helps increase visibility in the booth. They are available from most manufacturers of spray-booth equipment.

# Spray rooms

Don't let the considerable cost and space needed to set up a spray booth deter you from getting into spraying. When I first began spray finishing, my shop was one open room of about 800 sq. ft. I didn't have the space or money to set up a proper spray booth, but I needed an area that was well ventilated and relatively dust free. With a little creative effort I was able to build a spray room that functioned in much in the same way as a booth.

A spray room is an enclosed area that has an exhaust fan on one wall and an air-intake vent on another (see the drawing below). My room consisted of two simple 2x4 walls in the corner of the shop that framed out an area about 8 ft. by 10 ft. I used ½-in. plywood sheathing on the outside to give the walls some strength, and drywall on the inside. The drywall was taped and spackled, and all of the joints around the floor and air vents were caulked to help reduce dust infiltration. In one wall I installed a 6-ft. wide set of exterior doors that I salvaged off a remodeling job that were not only airtight, but also wide enough to allow for easy movement in and out of the room.

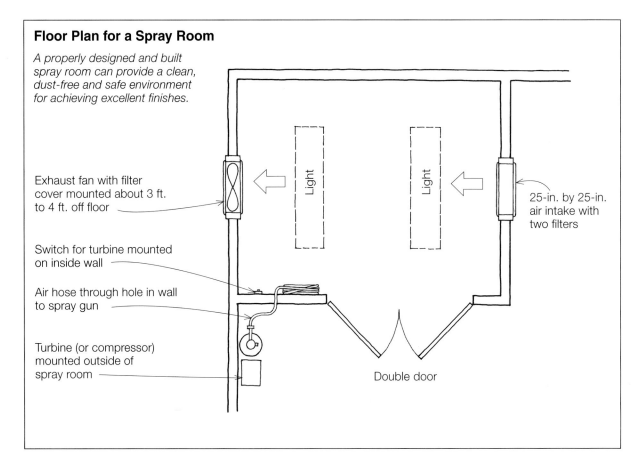

**Floor Plan for a Spray Room**

*A properly designed and built spray room can provide a clean, dust-free and safe environment for achieving excellent finishes.*

Exhaust fan with filter cover mounted about 3 ft. to 4 ft. off floor

Light

Light

25-in. by 25-in. air intake with two filters

Switch for turbine mounted on inside wall

Air hose through hole in wall to spray gun

Turbine (or compressor) mounted outside of spray room

Double door

Air flow was created through a simple ventilation system consisting of intake and exhaust openings. The intake vent was a hole in one wall, and the exhaust vent was an attic fan mounted in an opening in one of the exterior walls. In order to turn the fan off and on I removed the thermostat that usually controls it and wired the motor directly to a toggle switch. I mounted a louvered vent on the outside wall that opened whenever the fan was switched on, which helped keep rain from blowing through the fan and into the room.

Because I was spraying only water-based products, I did not need an explosion-proof fan; however, I was concerned that overspray would build up on the fan blades and motor and shorten its life, so I built a blast-gate type of housing around the unit. When the fan was in use, I slipped a filter into the slots around the opening, which did a good job of trapping the overspray before it could reach the fan. In winter, I would replace the filter with a piece of plywood when the fan was not in use to help reduce heat loss through the opening.

The air intake was simply a hole in the wall opposite the fan. I made this opening the same size as the blast gate that covered the fan so I could use the same size filters in both vents. Because dust control was a significant problem in my small shop, I covered the air-intake opening with two filters. A coarse furnace filter went into the slots on the out-side of the spray room, and a finer particle filter covered the opening on the inside wall. The combination of coarse and fine filters does a good job of removing most of the dust that could ruin a finish. When they became clogged, I would clean them with a blast of compressed air and reuse them several times before they became too flimsy.

Good lighting is essential to obtaining a good finish, so I installed an 8-ft. fluorescent light fixture in the ceiling and painted the walls and floor white. Finally, I set up the turbine for my HVLP system outside of the room and passed the hose into the spray area through a small hole in the wall. Having the turbine outside protected the motor from any over-spray and also reduced the noise in the small spray room. I plugged the turbine into an outlet that was operated by a switch inside the room so I could turn the system on and off without having to open the door.

Although my spray room was smaller than I wanted, the entire setup cost less than $300 and took about two days to build. Working quarters were tight, and I often found myself pressed against the walls as I tried to squeeze around a large cabinet. But the spray room was a great investment, given my limited space and money, and it paid for it-self in no time. Because I could spray my work in a relatively clean en-vironment, the room allowed me to offer better finishes than I had been. I also found that offering spray finishing as a service helped put me on equal footing with larger shops.

# Open rooms

Unfortunately, not all shops are large enough for a separate spray booth or room, so projects must be finished in the same place they are built. If this is the case with your shop, you may think that spraying is out of the question. But with a little care and extra work you will be able to get the same results as someone who has the luxury of a dedicated finishing area.

There is no doubt that spraying in the same room where you do your sawing and sanding involves more work than you'd have if you had a separate finishing area. However, spraying in a basement, garage or even outdoors is not a problem if you take a few precautions and pay careful attention to the cleanliness and air flow in your area.

As in a spray booth or finishing room, it's most important to circulate enough clean air through the area to remove potentially harmful vapors and prevent excessive buildup of overspray. Obviously, the more cross ventilation you have, the better, so always try to do your spraying in an area that has windows or doors on more than one wall. If you are spraying in a basement, position a fan in one window so it is blowing air through the room and out an opposite window. Take advantage of what the basement has to offer. If there are more than two windows, use another fan. Also, a fan or fans placed at key intervals along the floor will keep air moving and will help prevent overspray from collecting on the floor. If you plan on spraying in your basement, you should stay away from solvent-based finishes and nitrocellulose lacquers, which are toxic and highly flammable. Even if you have good air flow through the cellar, there is a chance that vapors could build up to the level where they could combust. The buildup of vapors is hazardous to your health and could cause problems not only for you but also for anyone living in the rooms above.

Although not perfect, garages are better suited for spraying than basements. Because garages are usually big, open spaces, circulating large amounts of air through them to remove the buildup of vapors and overspray is often fairly easy. In addition to overhead doors, most garages have a side or back entry or windows that can be opened to create natural cross ventilation. Placing a fan in the entry door or in one of the windows will further enhance the flow of air through the room. Because garages are open, the chance of vapors building up to a dangerous level is considerably less than it would be if you were spraying in a basement and will be less likely to cause health problems for the rest of your family.

**Spraying in a garage or outdoors should not present any problems, as long as you pick a warm, dry, and windless day.**

When given a choice between spraying in a garage or in a basement I would almost always choose the garage; however, spraying in a garage has a few drawbacks that must be considered. With the overhead doors open you are introducing a large amount of fresh air into the room, air that may be full of bugs, pollen, dust, leaves and so forth. A gust of wind could easily dump a handful of dandelion seeds right onto your freshly sprayed tabletop. To avoid such a disaster, don't spray on windy days. You can also try to limit wind-blown debris by leaving the overhead door partially closed. Although this will cut down on the amount of air flow, you should be able to find a compromise that allows an adequate air flow, yet still keeps out freshly cut grass and winged insects.

Unless you live in a warm climate, lack of heat can be a problem in a garage. Spraying a finish in 30°F weather is not only uncomfortable but also ineffective. The material becomes thick and stubborn and doesn't dry as it should. If you do have to spray in a garage during the winter months, you may want to heat it with an electric heater for a few hours before spraying, and then move the finished piece into the house as soon as it is dry enough to touch.

Whether you are spraying in a garage or in a basement, you should always make the area as clean as possible before you begin. If you cut, built and sanded your project in the room in which you will be spraying, there is probably dust covering everything. Getting rid of the dust before you spray will save you time and aggravation once you begin the finishing process. Give the entire room—including walls, shelves and equipment—a thorough cleaning with a heavy-duty shop vacuum well before you plan on spraying. Vacuuming ahead of time will allow any dust kicked up by the vacuum to settle onto the floor, which can be vacuumed again before you begin to spray. Sweeping compound, available at most hardware stores and lumberyards, does a good job of keeping down the dust on floors, and although it may seem like overkill, don't hesitate to use damp cloths, sponges or even a mop to pick up the finest dust.

Another drawback to spraying in your workshop is that once you begin you won't be able to do much else. Working on another project between coats would most likely create a cloud of dust that would prevent you from getting a smooth, blemish-free finish. It is better to accept the reality that you will have to leave the garage or basement after you have sprayed each coat and return when it is dry. This will not only keep down the dust but also give the room a chance to air out before you come back to work.

## Air sources

Once you have set up your spray area, whether it is an industrial booth, a spray room or just a garage or basement, you will need to locate and set up your turbine or compressor. If you are using compressed air to power your gun, you will have some work to do before you can begin spraying. If you have chosen a turbine-driven system, getting set up to spray is fairly simple.

### Turbines

All a turbine needs to operate is a 110v outlet and a location that will provide it with a source of clean air. Ideally your turbine should be placed in an area as far away as possible from the space in which you are spraying. A turbine draws in a large quantity of air, which, if filled with overspray, would quickly clog the filter and ruin the unit. Most HVLP systems come with 25-ft. hoses, so placing the turbine a distance from the spray gun shouldn't be a problem. Ideally, locate the turbine completely outside the spray room or booth to eliminate the possibility of overspray reaching the motor. If for some reason the only place you can put the turbine is near where you will be spraying, you may want to enclose it in a cabinet that has a filtered opening. In addition to limiting the amount of overspray that makes its way into the turbine, housing the turbine in a cabinet will also help dampen the noise.

What's most important when positioning your turbine, especially if it is inside a closed cabinet, is to give it plenty of breathing room. A turbine not only needs a good supply of clean air but will also exhaust warm air, especially if the unit has a bleeder valve, so be sure to allow plenty of space for proper ventilation. It is also a good idea to raise the turbine off the floor at least a foot or two. Gravity ensures that airborne debris will be most plentiful near the floor, so raising the unit will further reduce the risk of clogging the filter.

### Compressors

If you have a large air compressor in your shop you probably have most of the components that are needed to power a spray gun. Setting up a spray system may be a matter of tapping off an existing line and installing a drain and filter. However, if you are venturing into the world of air compressors for the first time, you should do a little research before spending any money on a system that may be too big or too small to suit your needs.

**If you do a lot of spraying or want to power other tools, you will need a fairly large compressor. This unit has a two-stage, 5-hp motor and an 80-gal. tank and takes up a fair amount of floor space.**

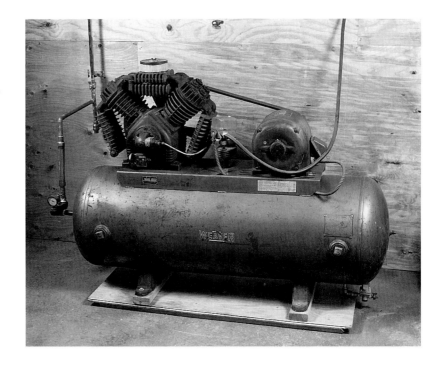

An air compressor that is powerful enough to run a spray system adequately can represent a considerable expense for the average hobbyist. In fact, I would be willing to bet that most professional small-shop owners thought twice before investing in a large air compressor. Choosing the right machine for your needs, and then properly setting up the entire system throughout your shop, may seem a bit daunting. It certainly won't be cheap.

Over time, the benefits of having a large compressor far outweigh the initial setup costs. Using compressed air to run your spray system gives you greater versatility in choosing and operating spray equipment and allows for greater production and better-quality finishes than can usually be achieved with a turbine-driven system. If you decide to use compressed air for your spraying, you get the extra benefit of having a compressor on hand for operating other equipment.

The first thing you must decide when setting up a compressed-air system is which compressor to use. A compressor consists of a motor that drives a pump that forces air into a storage tank. A piston inside the pump head draws air into the unit on the down stroke and compresses the air on the upstroke. As the air is compressed, the intake valve closes and the air is forced through an exhaust valve into the storage tank.

The 'head,' which sits on top of a compressor tank, is the heart of the unit. Air is drawn in through the filter on top, compressed by the pistons and moved into the tank for storage.

Not all compressors are created equal, and, as with most equipment, you get what you pay for. Smaller, inexpensive units usually consist of a single stage with one or more pistons of equal size. Because the air is compressed once, they operate efficiently only at lower pressures.

Compressors with larger motors and tanks will have two stages with two or more pistons of unequal size. In a two-stage compressor, air is first compressed in a large cylinder and then passed through a cooling unit into a second, smaller cylinder, where it is further compressed. In general, multi-stage units are heavy-duty machines that will provide large amounts of compressed air without working as hard. Because they are more efficient, they run cooler and deliver a greater amount of air for the power consumed.

Fortunately, comparing compressors is easy since they are all rated according to the air they deliver. This rating expresses the volume of air supplied per unit of time in cubic feet per minute (cfm) at a given pressure in pounds per square inch (psi). For example, I have a 5-hp compressor with an 80-gal. tank that is rated at 18 cfm at 175 psi (see the photo on the facing page). By comparison, my portable unit with a 1.5-hp motor and 4-gal. tank is rated at 4.7 cfm at 40 psi. Although this small unit delivers enough air to operate an HVLP touch-up gun

**Small, portable compressors are capable of delivering enough air to power spray guns for short periods of time and are handy for touch-up and repair work that must be done on a job site.**

for short times, it has nowhere near enough power to run the system I use in my shop. (A good way to determine the approximate cfm an electrically powered compressor can deliver is to multiply the horsepower of the motor by 4. Thus, a 5-hp compressor should be able to deliver somewhere around 20 cfm.)

Before you can choose a compressor, you must first decide how much air you need. Although small portable units can operate spray equipment, over time they simply will not be able to deliver enough air. If you plan on doing more than touch-up work you should have a compressor with at least a 3-hp motor. Anything smaller will not be able to keep up with a spray gun's constant demand for air. If you can afford a larger unit, I recommend that you look into something with a 5-hp motor and a 60-gal. to 80-gal. tank. This size compressor will not only run a spray system but will also be able to handle the air requirements of a host of other tools.

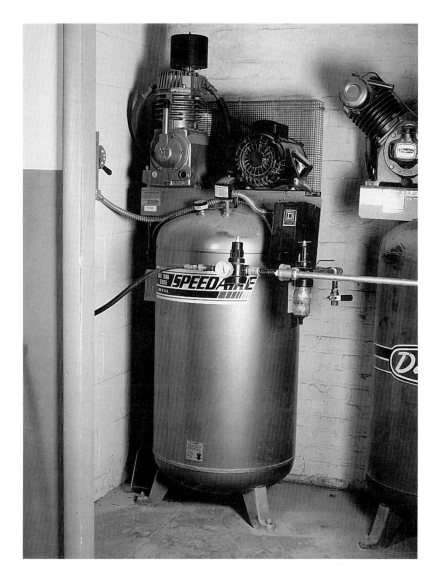

**Vertical compressors offer the same features as horizontal models but take up much less floor space.**

There are many brands, sizes and types of compressors on the market, some good and some not so good. Some sure signs of quality include a tank certified by the American Society of Mechanical Engineers (ASME) and cast-iron housings. The position of the tank (horizontal or vertical) is a matter of personal preference and the amount of space available. In an effort to lower costs, many manufacturers use a lot of aluminum and plastic in their products. If you don't plan on putting your compressor through continuous use, one of these less expensive models will work fine. However, if you are running a professional shop and expect maximum performance from your compressor for several years, it makes sense to invest in a heavy-duty industrial model.

However, the less expensive, lighter models offer certain advantages. In particular they may require less maintenance or have no oil to change. Any moving parts or belts are often protected by plastic covers, making them safe to be around in tight working quarters.

Heavy-duty compressors need to be watched closely. The large flywheel and belts are often exposed and could be quite dangerous in a busy shop. On my unit the belts are located on the back side of the motor so they are behind the unit, close to the wall. Even so, the risk that something or someone could get caught in them is very real. If you have a compressor like this, you should build a cage around it so nothing can come in contact with any of the moving parts.

*Maintenance*  Keeping the tank dry is without a doubt the most important part of maintaining a compressor, whatever its size. Moisture collecting in the bottom of the tank will not only make its way into the lines, but also will begin to corrode the walls of the tank itself. If too much moisture is left for a long time, scale forms, and the tank may deteriorate to the point where it either begins to leak or actually bursts.

Fortunately, it's easy to keep a compressor's storage tank dry, especially for smaller units. Opening the valve on the bottom of the tank will force whatever moisture has accumulated out of the tank. At the minimum, do this at the end of every day the compressor is used. On hot and humid days, you may have to drain the tank two or more times to keep the lines dry.

If you have a large compressor that is running all day, you may want to save yourself some work by installing an automatic drain valve on the tank. An automatic drain (see the photos on the facing page) is designed to open up briefly every time the pressure inside the tank drops by a certain amount, allowing a blast of air to escape. The valve on my compressor lets out a spit of wet air every time the pressure in the tank decreases by 10 psi. This valve saves me from having to drain the tank each day and also ensures that water is constantly being removed from the tank.

If you decide to install an automatic drain on your tank, be sure to check it occasionally to see if it is functioning properly. If your compressor is old or the tank is especially dirty, the drain valve may get stuck. It can usually be cleaned and reinstalled, but if your drain is getting clogged frequently, you may have to remove the valve and drain the tank manually.

If your compressor requires oil, be sure to change it on a regular basis, usually after about 100 hours of use. If I have been doing a lot of spraying, I change the oil on my compressor every three months. If I haven't been putting a great demand on the compressor, I may wait a little longer, but never more than six months.

In addition to clean oil, a compressor needs a clean air filter. If the air coming into the pump is dirty, the air going out to your gun will be dirty too. If you can, put your compressor outside of the work area so it won't suck in great quantities of wood dust. This will help keep the filter clean and also will reduce the amount of noise in your shop. Some compressors are so loud you can't carry on a conversation in the same room. I once worked in a shop that had two large, extremely loud units running about 30 minutes every hour. To keep from going insane we finally put mufflers on both of them, reducing the noise to acceptable levels.

As with most heavy equipment, new is not necessarily better. Good used compressors can usually be found at bargain prices. The unit I have in my shop is over 30 years old and cost me just $400 (compared with almost $4,000 for a comparable model today). All it needed was

**An automatic drain valve mounted on the bottom of a compressor tank eliminates the need to remove water manually at the end of the day and helps ensure a steady supply of dry air.**

**Automatic drains can become clogged with rust and scale and may need to be taken apart and cleaned frequently.**

an oil change, a new air filter and a little cleaning, and it was good as new. No matter what type of compressor you buy, keep it clean and well-maintained, and you should be rewarded with years of trouble-free operation.

## Air lines

Getting a steady supply of clean, dry air to the gun is critical for proper performance of the gun and the finishing material. Once you have your compressor firmly mounted on a level surface, run the lines that will carry the air to your spray gun. Improperly run air lines may cause problems once you begin spraying, and raw, untreated compressed air contains many contaminants that can ruin a finish. When air is compressed, moisture forms. Then, when warm compressed air hits cool metal air lines, further condensation takes place. Removing this water from the compressed air before it has a chance to become mixed into your finish material is of utmost importance, so every aspect of your air lines must be planned to force water away from the spray gun and back toward the compressor, where it can be easily drained. The drawing below shows a typical air-line setup.

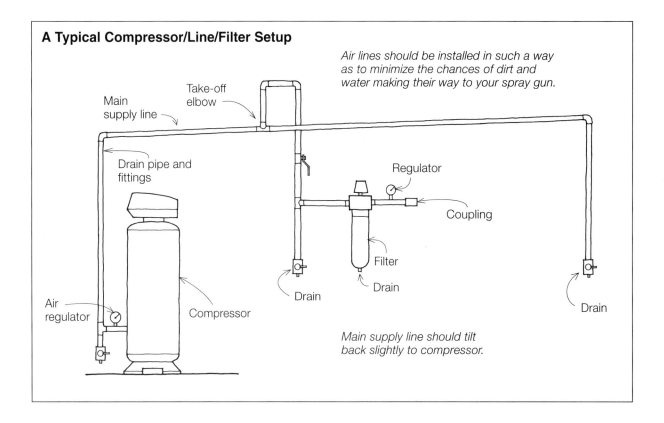

**A Typical Compressor/Line/Filter Setup**

*Air lines should be installed in such a way as to minimize the chances of dirt and water making their way to your spray gun.*

Take-off elbow

Main supply line

Drain pipe and fittings

Regulator

Coupling

Filter

Drain

Drain

Air regulator

Compressor

Drain

*Main supply line should tilt back slightly to compressor.*

**Put valves on both sides of the air take-off on a compressed-air system. The valve on top allows the air to be shut off if work has to be done on the line. The valve on the bottom drains water that builds up in the pipes.**

Run your main supply line straight up from the compressor as high as you can before carrying it across the ceiling to wherever it is needed. Try to slope the piping back toward the compressor, at least 1 in. for every 10 ft. A "take-off" or "drop" occurs at each location where you need a supply of air and should come from an elbow out of the *top* of the main supply line. When tapping into a compressed-air system it is a good idea to place valves on both sides of the air take-off (see the photo above). The valve on top allows the air to be shut off in case any work needs to be done on the line without having to close down and

| MINIMUM PIPE DIAMETERS FOR COMPRESSED-AIR LINES | | | |
|---|---|---|---|
| Compressor | | Main Air Line | |
| Power (hp) | Volume (cfm) | Length (ft.)* | Diameter (in.) |
| 1½ to 2 | 6 to 9 | 25 to 50 | ½ |
| | | Over 50 | ¾ |
| 3 to 5 | 12 to 20 | Up to 200 | ¾ |
| | | Over 200 | 1 |
| 5 to 10 | 20 to 40 | Up to 100 | ¾ |
| | | 100 to 200 | 1 |
| | | Over 200 | 1¼ |
| 10 to 15 | 40 to 60 | Up to 100 | 1 |
| | | 100 to 200 | 1¼ |
| | | Over 200 | 1½ |

*\* Always run air lines as directly as possible from the compressor to the gun.*
*Fittings are a source of pressure drop, so if you use a lot, you may want to increase the diameter of the pipe.*

bleed the whole system. The valve on the bottom serves as a drain for removing water that builds up in the pipes. The end of the main line should have a drain or valve as well.

The drop for your spray gun should be at least 25 ft. from the compressor so condensation can occur before the air reaches the gun. The more pipe you put between the compressor and your spray drop, the better. In my shop, air travels through about 75 ft. of pipe before it reaches the spray booth.

Whether you use copper or iron pipe doesn't make any difference, and what you use will be decided by its cost and your preference. Stay away from plastic pipe. PVC may be the cheapest alternative, but you will regret buying it when the lines begin to crack and the fittings start to leak. Most important, you should be sure the pipe is sized properly for your air source and for the length of the main line (see the charts above and on the facing page).

## RECOMMENDED HOSE SIZES FOR COMPRESSED-AIR SYSTEMS

|  | Length (ft.) | Inside diameter (in.) |
|---|---|---|
| **Air Hoses** | | |
| General Purpose | 0 to 12 | 1/4 |
|  | 12 to 100 | 5/16 |
| HVLP | 0 to 25 | 5/16 |
|  | 25 to 50 | 3/8 |
| **Fluid Hoses\*** | | |
| General Purpose | 1 to 25 | 3/8 |
|  | 25 to 100 | 1/2 |
|  | 100 to 200 | 3/4 |

*\*These specs are for fluid hoses at ground level. A fluid hose will lose 1/2 psi for every 1-ft. rise in elevation.*

## Filters

Even if all your lines are run properly and you drain your compressor's tank religiously, a small amount of water will still make its way to your spray drop. And worse, the air will probably contain impurities such as dirt, oil, scale or anything else that may be picked up from the tank or the lines. If you don't remove this foreign material, your finish will be less than perfect. A filter installed between the end of the piping and the hose that leads to the gun will ensure that the air making its way to your gun is as clean and dry as possible.

A filter, or "separator," is a self-contained unit that is mounted on the end of the air line to remove dirt and moisture from the air supply. As air enters the filter it is swirled around the inside of a canister or bowl, sending water particles out to the sides, where they fall to the bottom to be drained out of the system.

**A good filter system will remove most of the impurities that are carried through compressed-air lines. This unit consists of a water separator on the left and a coalescer on the right. Together they remove water and particles of dirt down to .01 microns in size.**

A good-quality separator is capable of removing particles as small as 5 microns. If your air is especially wet or dirty you may need to add a "coalescer." A coalescer is attached to the line after the separator (i.e., between the separator and the gun) and removes even smaller particles by sending the air through a filter of borosilicate glass microfibers. A good coalescer should be able to remove oil, water and dirt down to .01 microns and will come equipped with an automatic drain and an indicator that tells you when it is time to change the filter.

If a separator and coalescer aren't enough to get your air dry and clean, you can add a third stage to your system. A "dryer" contains chemical desiccants that reduce the amount of water in the air below the condensation, or dew, point. Like the coalescer, a dryer will have an indicator that lets you know when new desiccant is needed.

Finally, you can apply an in-line filter directly to your spray gun (see the photo on the facing page). These small, disposable units trap any water or dirt that may be left in the line before it reaches the gun. Although an in-line filter is not meant to replace the filtration system that is mounted to the air supply, it serves as extra insurance against contaminants in the finish. Although I don't use in-line filters when spraying in my shop, I have found them handy when using a touch-up gun with my portable, unfiltered compressor at a job site.

**An in-line filter is mounted directly to the end of the air hose as it enters the gun. Designed for limited use, these filters cost only a few dollars and are disposable.**

If you have a high-volume operation, you may find that a combination separator/coalescer/dryer still does not make the air as clean and dry as you would like. If that is the case, a larger, industrial-quality dryer will give you the ultimate in clean, dry air. These units can be fairly expensive and are designed for high volume, so unless you are a professional finisher who runs a spray gun all day, you will probably decide you can get by with the standard separators and coalescers.

There are dozens of filters, separators and coalescers on the market, and some of them work better than others. As with most things connected with spraying, it doesn't pay to skimp on quality. Saving a few dollars on a cheap filter is hardly worth the cost of having to refinish something that has been ruined by a contaminated finish. If you stick with filtration units that are designed specifically for spray finishing and avoid generic "air-tool" devices, you should be able to create and maintain a reliable supply of clean, dry air.

# Safety equipment

No spray setup is complete without some safety equipment. Because spraying releases fine clouds of mist and vapors into the air, it creates respiratory and fire hazards not generally associated with brushing or wiping on finishes. Whether you are working in a large spray booth or your basement, you should be sure to take the proper precautions, especially if you are spraying highly toxic or flammable materials such as nitrocellulose lacquers. However, it is a mistake to think that if you work only with water-based products you don't need to be careful. Just because they are labeled nontoxic doesn't mean you should coat your lungs with them.

### Respirators

For most finishing operations a regular paint-spray, or organic-vapor, respirator is all you need. These large, twin-cartridge face masks (see the photo below) have a heavy, rubber face piece and two head straps. A good-quality paint respirator will contain two filter elements: a prefilter, which traps large airborne particles, and a chemical or charcoal cartridge filter, which absorbs finer mists and vapors.

Because the prefilter catches the larger particles of overspray, it tends to get dirty fairly quickly. Fortunately, the paper or cloth filter replacements are relatively inexpensive, so there is no excuse for not replacing a pair as soon as they become dirty. Failure to keep the prefilters clean will shorten the life of the cartridges, which are much more expensive. I buy my prefilters in bulk boxes so I always have plenty.

**An organic vapor mask traps potentially harmful vapors in a charcoal cartridge. The cartridge and paper prefilter can be removed and disposed of when they become full.**

The cartridges on your respirator should last through several changes of prefilters before they too need to be replaced. Deciding when to change the prefilters is easy, especially if you spray a lot of dark-colored paints and stains, because you can see when they are dirty. In order to determine when to change the cartridge filters you will have to depend on your nose, rather than your eyes. When you can smell the material you are applying, the cartridges have absorbed all they can and need to be changed immediately. If you happen to have a cold and can't smell anything, you will still be able to tell the cartridges need to be changed because you will start to get a funny taste on your lips and in the back of your throat.

You should change the cartridges as soon as you have the slightest indication they are becoming dirty. Wearing a respirator that is not working is pretty much the same as not wearing one at all, so don't try to squeak a few extra days out of a dirty mask. I always keep extra cartridges on hand so I don't have to interrupt my finishing schedule when they need to be changed.

If wearing a respirator with dirty filters and cartridges is bad, wearing one that doesn't fit is worse. Leaks around the rubber face piece allow harmful mists and vapors to pass directly to your nose and mouth, which defeats the purpose of wearing the respirator. At first, getting a proper fit with a new mask may be a bit difficult and even uncomfortable, but after the rubber has softened, you will have an easier time pulling it tightly to your face. One good way to tell if you have an airtight seal around your mouth and nose is to put your hand over the exhalation valve and blow out a gentle, but firm, puff of air. If you can feel air escaping around the sides of the mask, it is not on properly and needs to be adjusted. If you have to blow pretty hard to get air to escape, you have the mask on correctly. If you have a beard, a standard respirator won't fit properly, so be sure to get one designed for people with beards.

Wearing a respirator can be a little uncomfortable, especially on hot days. In order to get mine to fit properly I have to pull the two head straps pretty tight. Usually, by the end of the day, I have a severe case of "mask face." When I take the respirator off, the outline of it stays with me for quite a while. This invariably causes great amusement with my shop mates, but I think it is a small price to pay for protecting my lungs.

If you do a lot of spraying, protecting your skin and clothes may become an issue, especially if you do not have a good ventilation system. Even with proper ventilation, overspray tends to settle not only on the

**Check your mask for an airtight fit each time you put it on. There are even masks designed specifically for people who have beards.**

Even if you have taken all the necessary precautions, some overspray is bound to find its way onto your clothes. These sneakers, which used to be black, were ruined after only a few hours of spraying white lacquer.

walls and floors, but also on your head, clothes and shoes (see the photo at left). When I first began spraying, I would carry this over-spray around with me and eventually deposit it in my house at the end of the day. After ruining countless pairs of pants, shirts, shoes and even glasses, I came to the conclusion that I would need a special suit, or uniform, to be worn only when spraying. Today, I wear the same pair of glasses, sneakers and painter's jumpsuit whenever I spray. I wear the glasses home with me, but the shoes and suit stay in the shop. This way my house and I stay cleaner, and the amount of dust that can travel into my spray booth is limited. After working at the table saw on one project, I can brush myself off, put on the clean suit that hangs in the finishing room, and step into the spray booth without worrying about covering my clothes with overspray or the finished piece with dust.

## Fire extinguishers

It is a good idea to check with your local building officials before setting up a spray booth, since they may require you to install a fire suppression or sprinkler system. If you spray only water-based materials, you may be able to get away without one. If not, ask if you have the option to use either a dry chemical or water-sprinkler system. Given the choice, I would use a chemical system for two reasons. Because it is a self-contained unit, you do not have to run water lines to your spray booth, which could get costly, especially if the only source of water isn't close to the booth, or if you have to pay a plumber to do the work for you.

The second, and more important, reason I would recommend a dry chemical system is that there is less chance of an expensive chemical cleanup if it is ever activated. If a sprinkler system goes off, water could make its way into the street, or worse, into the town's sewer or water system. Your local municipality may not take too kindly to having the streets or water system contaminated with chemicals that have washed off the walls and floor of your spray booth, and may require you to foot the bill for any cleanup.

A dry chemical system is less of a potential environmental and financial risk. If the system is ever activated, it will certainly make a mess. However, the residue can be cleaned up and disposed of properly without contaminating the surrounding area.

If you are spraying in a small room, a garage or your basement, you won't need an expensive fire-suppression system, but this does not mean that there is no risk of fire. In fact, spraying in a small area that may have less than ideal ventilation increases the potential for fire. You should always keep at least one fire extinguisher within easy reach, wherever you spray.

**Fire extinguishers in good working condition, like this dry chemical extinguisher (left) and water extinguisher (right), are essential spray-finishing accessories.**

A good-quality fire extinguisher is relatively inexpensive when compared with the potential losses associated with fire, so don't try to save a few bucks by buying a small model meant for kitchen grease fires. In my shop I have both a 6-lb. dry chemical unit and a 2½-gal. water extinguisher (see the photos above), which together cost around $200. I am on a regular maintenance schedule with the company that sold me the units. For $20 a year they send someone to my shop annually to inspect and, if necessary, recharge the extinguishers. Local codes require that I have a valid inspection sticker on all my extinguishers, but even if they didn't I would still get them inspected each year. Luckily, I have never had to use either of them, but knowing they are there and functioning properly is a comfort.

# CHAPTER 4
# The Basics of Spray Finishing

Once you have chosen a system and set up a spray booth or finishing area, you are ready to begin spraying. Spraying a good-quality finish is easy and doesn't require a great deal of time or effort; however, there is more to do than simply pouring some finish into the cup, turning on the compressor or turbine and spraying. In order to achieve a smooth, even coat that is free of dust, blemishes, runs, drips, orange peel and other defects, you must prepare the gun and the material before you begin to spray. The finish should be thinned to the proper viscosity, the gun must be clean and properly loaded, the air flow and fan pattern must be adjusted to fit the object being finished and the mechanics of spraying must be smooth and consistent.

## Thinning the material

It would certainly make life easy if you could just pour your finish straight from the can into a spray gun and begin applying it without any other preparations. Depending on the material being used and the type of spray system you have, this will usually be possible. Sometimes, however, you will have to thin the material in order to achieve a smooth, even finish that flows together properly. The thickness of a material is referred to as its "viscosity," which is actually a measurement of the internal friction among the molecules of the liquid as they flow past each other. Thinning the material lowers its viscosity, lightening it so it can be atomized into smaller particles, which then flow together to give a smooth, even appearance. The trick to thinning is

Various thinners are designed to work with different finish materials. Thinners may be toxic, like lacquer and paint thinner, flammable, like denatured alcohol, or perfectly harmless, like the jug of water on the right.

knowing how much thinner to add. If the material is too heavy or thick it won't atomize properly, and you will get a rough, bumpy film; if it's too thin, a host of other problems can result.

First, of course, you must determine what to use as a thinning agent. Most manufacturers will list the appropriate thinner on the can of finish material, and it is always a good idea to use the recommended thinner. Never substitute a different thinner unless you are sure it will give the same results. Occasionally, a label will say the material does not need to be thinned and will not tell you what to use if you need to thin it. A good guideline is to use whatever material is recommended to clean up. In other words, if the can says to clean brushes or spray equipment with mineral spirits, use that as a thinner. Most water-based products have special thinners, or "flow additives," but in a pinch, small amounts of water can be used.

Once you have selected the appropriate thinner, you will need to determine how much to use. Sometimes the manufacturer will tell you, which eliminates any guesswork. In many cases, however, there will be no indication of quantity, so you will have to follow general guidelines that apply to the type of material (as opposed to the specific brand) and the equipment being used.

Some spray-gun manufacturers will indicate how much the material should be thinned when using a particular needle/tip combination. This information may be given as a straight ratio or percentage of thinner to finish or may be expressed as the number of seconds it takes to empty a viscosity cup, a device designed to measure viscosity. A viscosity cup (see the photo at right) has a small hole in the bottom that

A viscosity cup is used to gauge the thickness of a finish material before spraying. Comparing the time it takes for the cup to empty with the finish manufacturer's recommendation will give you an indication of how much, if any, thinner to add.

# VISCOSITY-CUP CONVERSION CHART

| Zahn #1 | Zahn #2 | Fischer #1 | Fischer #2 | Ford Cup #3 | Ford Cup #4 |
|---|---|---|---|---|---|
| 30 | 16 | 20 | | | 5 |
| 34 | 17 | 25 | | | 8 |
| 37 | 18 | 30 | 15 | 12 | 10 |
| 41 | 19 | 35 | 17 | 15 | 12 |
| 44 | 20 | 39 | 18 | 19 | 14 |
| 52 | 22 | 50 | 21 | 25 | 18 |
| 60 | 24 | | 24 | 29 | 22 |
| 68 | 27 | | 29 | 33 | 25 |
| | 30 | | 33 | 36 | 28 |
| | 34 | | 39 | 41 | 31 |
| | 37 | | 44 | 45 | 32 |
| | 41 | | 50 | 50 | 34 |
| | 49 | | 62 | 58 | 41 |
| | 58 | | | 66 | 45 |
| | 66 | | | | 50 |
| | 74 | | | | 54 |
| | 82 | | | | 58 |

*The numbers in this chart refer to the time in seconds it takes the cup to empty.*

allows liquid to drain through. When a cupful empties within the prescribed time range, you know the material is thinned to the correct viscosity for your equipment. There are several different brands and sizes of viscosity cup. The chart on the facing page will allow you to thin your material using whatever cup you might have.

Besides viscosity, other factors such as temperature and humidity can affect how well a material sprays, so whatever method of thinning you use will no doubt include a certain amount of trial and error. Even if you follow the finish material or spray-gun manufacturer's instructions exactly, you may have to adjust the ratio of thinner to finish to suit your particular needs.

Thinning most finish materials is simple, but there are certain procedures to follow in order to ensure consistency from one application to the next and to avoid potential problems. First, get some measuring equipment (see the photo below). Purchase a set of measuring cups with easy-to-read markings along with a set of measuring spoons and a shot glass or two. These don't have to be high-quality chemist's tools; ordinary kitchen gear will do. In fact, I use cheap plastic stuff from a

**Mixing finishes doesn't call for sophisticated tools. An inexpensive set of plastic measuring spoons and a couple of measuring cups and shot glasses are all you will need for most applications.**

## FINISHING LOG

PROJECT: **Shoe Stool**          DATE: 9/10/95

**FINISH MATERIALS:**

STAIN/PAINT: 1 Part Hydrocote NGR dye "Provincial Walnut"
1 Part Hydrocote NGR dye "Maple"

SEALER: M.L. Campbell Sanding Sealer

TOPCOAT: M.L. Campbell "Ultrastar" clear gloss lacquer

| SPRAY SCHEDULE: | NOTES: |
|---|---|
| 1 - Spray 1st coat dye | Dry 1 hour |
| 2 - Spray 2nd coat dye | " " " |
| 3 - Spray moderate coat sealer | Dry 30 minutes |
| 4 - Sand | 320-grit wet/dry paper |
| 5 - Spray 1st coat lacquer | Dry 2 hours |
| 6 - Sand | 400 grit |
| 7 - Spray 2 coats lacquer | Let dry 1 hour between coats |

EQUIPMENT USED:  Dye - { AccuSpray gun w/ .043 tip
Sealer - { and #7 air cap.
Lacquer - .051 tip w/ #9 air cap

RESULTS/COMMENTS:
Lacquer was thinned 5% w/ "Aquaflow"

local variety store. The key when mixing thinner and paint is to make accurate measurements and keep good records. Every time I finish something I record the materials and methods used in a log book (see the illustration on the facing page). Detailed notes help when I have to repair old jobs, and they also serve as a handy reference when I need to recreate a finish or color for a new project. Consistency in finishing is important, and keeping detailed notes on the temperature, humidity and ratio of thinner to paint will allow you to recreate a successful finish time after time. Once you have found the ideal mixture for your set-up, you certainly don't want to have to reinvent it a month later.

## Common thinning problems

Using too much thinner can cause a number of problems. It may lower the viscosity of the finish material to the point where it atomizes too much, resulting in a fine mist that actually dries before it coats the surface—a condition called "dry spray." If the viscosity of the material is reduced too much, it may flow so easily (especially on vertical surfaces) that it runs, drips or sags. Too much thinner may also lengthen the drying time, thereby slowing down production and also allowing dust to settle on the finish, causing even more trouble.

Thinner may also lighten or dilute the color of paint or colored lacquers so much that they lose their ability to hide the underlying wood, thereby requiring the application of more coats than would otherwise be necessary to build the desired color. In fact, too much thinner in a colored top coat may reduce its depth of color and opacity, so that no matter how many coats you apply you will never achieve the desired results. Also, pinprick-sized bubbles (called "solvent pop") may form on the surface of the object as an excessive amount of thinner tries to escape from the rapidly drying finish.

Finally, excess thinner also reduces the "build" capabilities of a finish, so more coats may have to be applied to achieve the same film thickness, depth or shine than would have been achieved with less thinner.

On the other hand, if you don't use enough thinner, the material may not break up into drops small enough to flow together on the surface of the wood. As a result, the applied finish will be coarse or lumpy and will resemble the skin of an orange, a condition known as "orange peel."

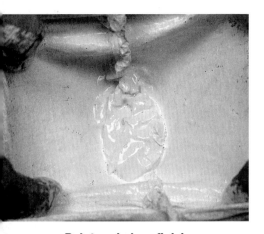

Paint and clear finishes, especially water-based products, are never as clean as they look. This large glob of primer was left after two gallons were run through the strainer.

## Filling the gun

Once the finish material is prepared for spraying, you are ready to fill the cup or pot. Obviously you want your equipment to be as clean as possible, since a speck of dirt or dried paint could ruin your finish. You also want the material being sprayed to be as clean as possible. Although you probably won't notice them, small particles of dust, dirt, hair, wood chips, brush bristles and other foreign matter can easily collect in a can of finish. As a result, the finish must be "cleaned" just as the gun is.

Cleaning the finish involves pouring it through a strainer, which will remove any impurities that may have gathered. There are many types of strainers (see the photo below), all of which work to varying extents. Some of the most common are nylon mesh or paper funnels that have small holes in the bottom. The nylon strainers (see the bottom photo on the facing page) are slightly more expensive than the paper ones but can be cleaned and reused indefinitely. Although the paper filters can also be cleaned and reused, they do not last very long, and cleaning them without causing any damage is somewhat difficult. I have seen cheesecloth recommended as a strainer, but I think the holes are too large to remove the tiny particles that could ruin a finish.

Strainers come in various sizes and shapes. The kitchen strainer in the center works well with a 1-qt. or 2-qt. cup. For larger containers, you can use a mesh 'stocking' like the one at right. The paper filter at left is inexpensive but can be used only a few times at best before it falls apart.

Another alternative is to use plastic kitchen-type strainers. These are cups with a piece of tight nylon mesh in the bottom and a handle on the side. I have been using the same one for over two years without any problems. Because it is plastic it is easy to clean, and it fits right into the top of my 1-qt. cup, so both of my hands are free. Also, it is a lot less messy to use than flimsy nylon and paper filters.

It doesn't matter what type of strainer you use as long as it is fine enough to capture the smallest particles of dirt and dust while still allowing the paint to flow through. Simply place the strainer over your cup or pot and pour in the paint. Make a habit of always cleaning the strainer immediately after use. Otherwise, the finish will dry and clog the holes in the filter, making it extremely difficult to get clean.

As an added precaution you may want to place an internal filter on the tip of the fluid tube inside the gun. Sometimes called "worthy screens," these filters (see the photo at right) are designed to remove any particles or clots that may have been missed by your initial straining. Although they are inexpensive (around $5 apiece) and seem like a good idea, I have never felt the need for one. So long as your equipment is clean and you are careful to strain the material properly, you should have no problems with contaminants once the gun is loaded and sealed for spraying.

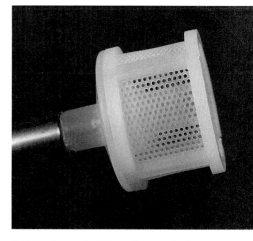

**A filter inserted into the end of the fluid tube further reduces the chance of foreign particles working their way into the gun or finish coats.**

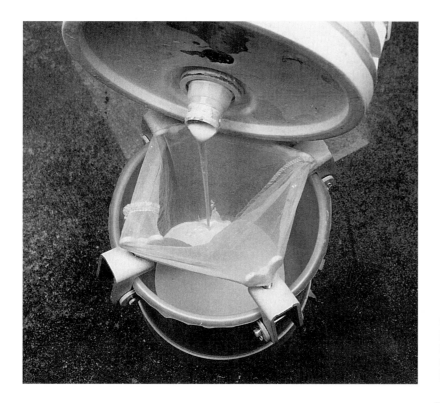

**A large nylon-mesh filter fits perfectly over the clamps on a 2½-gal. pressure pot, freeing up both hands for pouring large buckets of finish.**

## Selecting a fluid tip and air cap

Before you begin spraying you must be sure the gun is properly out-fitted for the finish material being used. This is especially true for HVLP spraying, since the air cap must work in conjunction with the fluid tip for proper atomization. If the fluid tip and needle are the wrong size for the material being sprayed, the resulting finish may be too thick or too thin. The wrong air cap may not atomize the material into small enough droplets, or it may break them up so finely that they dry before they can flow together on the surface being sprayed. If you understand the relationship between the fluid needle, tip and air cap on an HVLP system, you'll find it much easier to lay down an even, wet coat of finish material that flows together smoothly.

In a turbine-driven HVLP system, the amount of air being fed to the gun is constant, so any adjustment in fluid and air flow must be made first by selecting the proper needle, tip and air cap and then by setting the air and fluid needles on the gun. Choosing the proper tip and air cap may be a bit tricky because the type of material being sprayed di-rectly affects your choice. Fortunately, most HVLP gun manufacturers will specify in the instructions that come with the gun what combina-tion they recommend for each type of material.

You may need to change the setup for certain applications, so you need to understand what each component does. The fluid tip controls the amount of material that is fed into the atomizing air stream. In gen-eral, lighter material will flow more easily, so you need a smaller tip. Thicker materials, or materials with a higher percentage of solids, will require larger fluid tips.

The air cap controls the velocity of the air as it leaves the gun and de-termines how finely the fluid is atomized. Atomization takes place as air passes through the center, or annular, hole and is directed into the

**If you spray a variety of materials you may have to adjust the size of the fluid needle and tip, or switch to a different air cap. Having several setups on hand allows you to use the same gun to spray just about any type of finish.**

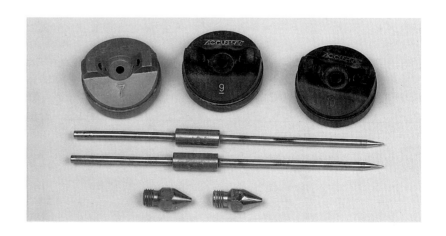

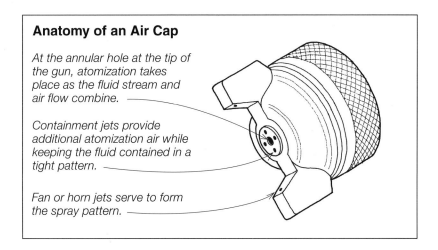

**Anatomy of an Air Cap**

*At the annular hole at the tip of the gun, atomization takes place as the fluid stream and air flow combine.*

*Containment jets provide additional atomization air while keeping the fluid contained in a tight pattern.*

*Fan or horn jets serve to form the spray pattern.*

fluid stream (see the drawing above). The holes in smaller air caps decrease in size and therefore force the flow of air through the tip of the gun at a higher velocity, creating finer atomization. In theory, the smaller the air cap, the finer the finish. However, if an air cap gets too small for the material being used, the velocity of the air will be too great, breaking the finish into particles that are so fine they actually dry before they are deposited on the surface being sprayed. If this "dry spray" occurs, you can try moving the gun closer to the surface, but you will probably get better results if you switch to a larger air cap.

Most HVLP guns come equipped with a standard setup that is appropriate for most finishing materials—usually a fluid tip that measures between .050 in. and .055 in. in diameter along with the corresponding air cap. This tip will provide good fluid flow for most standard materials, including latex paint, and will give an acceptable finish most of the time. If you find that this setup does not give you the results you expect, try a different combination of fluid tip and air cap until you get a good finish (and note what works in your log). In fact, if you do a lot of spraying, you will probably come to own several different fluid tips and air caps.

## Adjusting the gun

Once you have selected a fluid tip and air cap and have strained the material into the cup, you are ready to adjust the controls on the gun to begin spraying. How you proceed depends on whether your system is turbine driven or compressor driven, as discussed on pp. 78-79. As you make adjustments, it's a good idea to run a test on a piece of scrap wood or cardboard so you can do any further tweaking before actually spraying your piece.

### Turbine-driven HVLP

Adjusting a turbine-driven HVLP gun is simple. Begin by turning both the fluid-adjustment knob and fan- or air-adjustment knob all the way off. Open the air-adjustment knob a little, about a quarter of a turn, and then depress the trigger. As the air is rushing out of the gun, open the fluid-adjustment knob until the material begins to flow. Continue turning the fluid-adjustment knob until the spray becomes a full, wet coat. From this point you can adjust both knobs in conjunction with each other to obtain the optimal spray rate and fan pattern.

The type of material being sprayed, the size of the object to be coated and the desired application speed will play a role in determining how you adjust the fluid and air controls. If you want to lay down a lot of material in a hurry, you will need to open the fluid control more. If you are coating large surfaces, you will want to increase the air flow to widen the fan pattern as much as possible. On the other hand, if you are trying to achieve a really fine finish or are working on small objects, you will get better results by restricting the air and fluid flows, thereby gaining better control over how much material is sprayed and where it lands.

It's important to remember when adjusting the fluid and air controls that the position of one knob directly affects the setting of the other (see the photo below). For example, if you increase the air flow without adjusting the fluid flow, the finish material may come out too fine and won't coat the surface properly. Conversely, opening the fluid control without increasing the air flow or fan size may result in too much material hitting the surface too quickly, thereby causing runs,

**Viewed from left to right, these test patterns show the effects of adjusting the air and fluid control knobs. The wide, light band on the left was made with the air flow fully open and the fluid flow almost completely closed. As the air flow is restricted and the fluid control simultaneously opened, the pattern gets tighter and darker. The solid line of paint at far right was made by closing the air control all the way and opening the fluid control as far as it can go.**

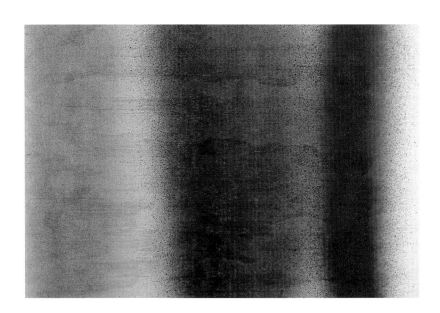

drips and sags. Determining the ideal settings is mostly a matter of trial and error and may take time to learn. You will know you have the right settings when the finish material coats the surface evenly and flows together smoothly.

Once you've determined the right settings for the material being sprayed, make a note of them (most guns have index lines on the knobs) so you can quickly return to the same settings at a later date.

### Compressor-driven HVLP

Setting the fluid flow and air-pattern adjustments on a conversion or compressed-air HVLP gun follows the same rules and principles explained above for a turbine-driven system. However, because the gun is using compressed air, you will have another set of controls to adjust in order to ensure proper material flow and atomization. You will need to regulate the air pressure coming into the gun handle. This should be done either at the compressor or at a fluid pressure regulator (see the photo at right) that is attached to the line between the gun and the compressor, and should be set according to the manufacturer's recommendation for the particular air cap being used.

Once you have the required pressure coming into the gun, you can begin adjusting the fluid pressure, fluid flow and fan pattern. Begin by turning the fluid- and fan-control knobs all the way open and the fluid-pressure regulator all the way closed. While pulling the gun trigger, you can begin increasing the fluid pressure by slowly opening the fluid-regulator knob until you achieve good paint flow. If too much material is being sprayed, turn the regulator knob all the way down, release the pressure from the cup by depressing the poppet, or check valve, and begin the process again.

If you are using a remote pressure pot on a compressed-air HVLP gun, the fluid pressure control is already mounted on the tank. As a result, you must remove the fluid pressure regulator from the gun handle and plug the hole with a cap (see the photo at right).

Since you have to set the fluid-regulator knob to control the pressure of the fluid as it flows to the tip, adjusting the gun is a little more difficult than adjusting a turbine-driven system. Instead of having two adjustments to coordinate (fluid and air flow), you have three. Getting the air flow, fluid flow and fluid pressure working together to give you the proper rate of even, well-atomized coverage is tricky and will take some trial and error. However, having this extra adjustment makes a compressed-air HVLP gun extremely versatile and gives you many more options than you have with a turbine-driven system.

**Some compressed-air HVLP systems have a fluid pressure regulator mounted right on the handle of the gun. Adjusting the knob on the regulator controls how fast the fluid enters the atomizing air stream and allows for greater control over application rates.**

**When using a remote pressure pot on a compressed-air HVLP gun, you must remove the fluid pressure regulator and plug the hole with a cap.**

## Spraying: general techniques

At last the material is strained and loaded and the gun is properly adjusted; you are finally ready to spray. Using a spray gun is not very difficult, but there are some general techniques to master, and it may take an hour or two of practice before you feel comfortable aiming the gun at a fine piece of furniture and pulling the trigger.

It is always a good idea to practice on a piece of scrap wood or cardboard to double-check your settings and finish material before working on the piece to be finished. I like to tape a scrap of heavy paper or cardboard on the wall to use for testing; it's convenient and easy to dispose of, and it helps keep the spray booth clean.

**Spraying the underside of a shelf or into tight corners can be awkward at first, but gets easier with practice.**

A turntable or lazy Susan is one of the most valuable accessories to any spray system. (The one shown here is viewed from the bottom.) Don't make the top of the turntable too large, or it will be in the way when you try to spray small objects. A lip attached to the top overhangs the mechanism to protect it from becoming clogged with overspray.

To achieve even coverage, follow these simple guidelines, which apply regardless of the size and shape of the object being sprayed:

• Place the workpiece on rollers or a turntable so it can be moved with minimum effort. (Larger objects can be propped up on sawhorses.) Standing in one place and moving the piece will ensure that you are always spraying in the same direction; body motions that could result in an inconsistent or jerky spray pattern will be kept to a minimum. Since you always want to be spraying toward the fan or exhaust system, it is better to shift the workpiece than to move around it.

• Keep all of your motions as smooth, consistent and controlled as possible. Place the piece at a comfortable height so you can spray without having to bend, reach or otherwise contort your arm or body while spraying.

• Hold the gun perpendicular to the work surface at all times. Keep it the same distance from the workpiece for the entire length of the pass, and move it smoothly across the piece, without any changes in speed.

If you fail to follow any one of these guidelines, the coverage will be uneven, with some areas receiving too much spray and others not enough. If you fail to follow two or even all three, you will greatly compound the problem of uneven coverage and may end up with pools of material and runs in one spot while other areas may be starved for finish.

## The mechanics of spraying

When you spray, move your arm in a wide, sweeping motion. Remember that the motion is in your arm and not in your body. Your hand must be held as still as possible while your arm carries the gun in a straight, unswerving line across the object. This movement may seem a little awkward and even tiring at first, but with a little practice it will soon become second nature.

The best way to obtain a smooth, even spray pattern is to start your arm motion before the gun is over the object on one side and continue it until the gun is past the other side. Trigger the gun a split second after you start your motion, and keep spraying until your arm stops. Doing this may seem like a waste of material, since you are beginning and ending each pass by spraying into the air; however, the material lost is a small price to pay for complete coverage from one side of the piece to the other. In general, you should begin your motion about 6 in. from one side and finish the same distance from the other side. With practice you will get a good feel for the gun, and you will be better able to judge when to squeeze the trigger and when to release it, thereby maximizing efficiency.

For a flat surface, move the gun in a straight line across the piece (see the drawing on the facing page). Swinging your arm in an arc will result in an uneven coat, as will tilting the gun when spraying a vertical surface. The gun should be held at the same distance from the workpiece through the entire spraying motion (see the drawing on p. 84). For compressed-air systems hold the gun 8 in. to 10 in. away. Because the mist created by HVLP systems is much softer, you must move the gun closer to the surface, or the material may dry before it reaches its target. For HVLP spraying, 6 in. to 8 in. away from the work should yield a full, wet coat with minimal overspray. (Keep in mind that these guidelines may not be exactly right for every application.) Once you have gained some experience and are familiar with your equipment and materials, you can adjust the distance between the gun and the workpiece to get better control of the rate of application.

Before you begin spraying, adjust the gun so it will be laying down the widest fan possible with the least amount of overspray (see pp. 77-79). This will, of course, vary with the size and shape of the piece, but in general you want to be able to cover the entire object with the least number of passes. When spraying small objects or into tight places, you may find that restricting the flow of material a little and moving the gun closer to the surface will give you better control. Large areas may be covered more quickly by increasing the flow of material and pulling the gun back an inch or two.

# Basic Spray Technique

### Correct

*Move the gun in a straight line, holding it at the same distance from the workpiece for the entire pass. Maintaining a flexible wrist helps keep the tip of the gun parallel to the surface being sprayed.*

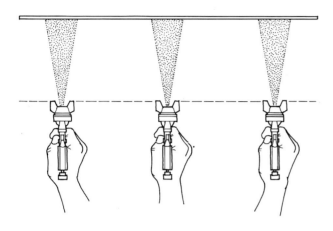

### Incorrect

*Moving the gun in an arc across the workpiece will result in uneven coverage: too much material in the middle and not enough at the edges.*

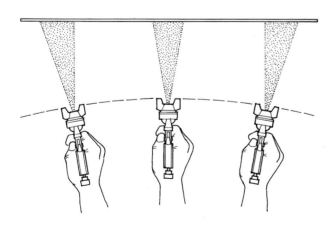

## Optimum Distance from Workpiece

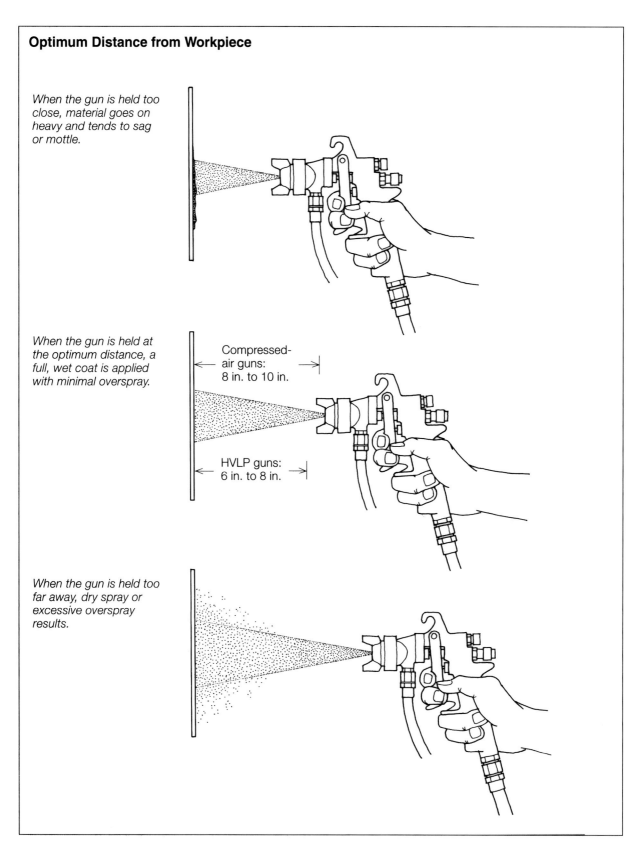

When the gun is held too close, material goes on heavy and tends to sag or mottle.

When the gun is held at the optimum distance, a full, wet coat is applied with minimal overspray.

Compressed-air guns: 8 in. to 10 in.

HVLP guns: 6 in. to 8 in.

When the gun is held too far away, dry spray or excessive overspray results.

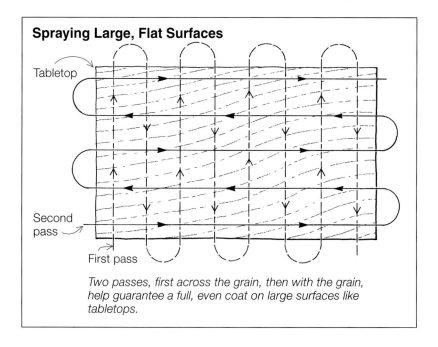

**Spraying Large, Flat Surfaces**

Tabletop

Second pass

First pass

*Two passes, first across the grain, then with the grain, help guarantee a full, even coat on large surfaces like tabletops.*

Once you have found the optimum distance from the surface, you should hold the gun at that point with as little variation as possible. Move the gun evenly across the surface at about the same speed you would move a brush. If you find the finish material is going on either too light or too heavy, slow down or speed up your motion until you have adequate coverage. Each pass should overlap the previous one by about half, which will help prevent any thin spots or complete misses. On large surfaces such as case sides or tabletops, I like to make two passes in opposite directions. First I lightly spray a tack coat across the grain, and then I go back immediately and spray a slightly heavier coat with the grain (see the drawing above). These two passes form one full coat that is uniform in thickness and coverage.

**Organizing your work**

Although the order in which you spray the parts of a particular piece will depend on its size and shape, there are certain rules that apply in any situation. For instance, always try to work so that you are moving the gun away from your body and toward the exhaust fan. This will help prevent overspray from settling on areas that have already been sprayed; it will also give you a better view of the piece you are spraying and will result in a cleaner work environment.

Before spraying a piece of furniture it is usually a good idea to make a dry run through the entire process. This approach allows you to visualize the steps you'll need to take and prevents overcoating or missing any areas. Start with the least visible areas (drawer bottoms, cabinet backs, etc.) and work your way toward those parts that will be seen. Doing the most visible areas last allows you to work carefully around any spots that may have been covered when spraying adjacent sections, and will result in a uniform coat where it matters most. For example, you should always spray the edges of tabletops, doors or shelves before working on the top surfaces (see the photos below). This not only builds a thicker finish on the sharp corners (where you would be likely to cut through the finish when sanding), but also allows you to even out the material that lands on the perimeter of the top by feathering a light pass over it, thereby creating a uniform coating that will flow together evenly over the entire panel.

The drawing on the facing page describes the order of work for spraying a cabinet. Spraying tight areas such as the insides of cabinets and drawers can be a problem, especially if they are hard to reach. To avoid creating a cloud of overspray or bounce back when working in tight areas, it helps to cut back on the flow of material and work from the corners out. In tight areas you will use more wrist motion than you would when spraying flat surfaces, and you will need a quicker finger on the trigger. Similarly, areas where two passes may overlap, such as the joint between a stretcher and the leg of a chair, must be sprayed carefully. Avoid getting too thick a coat, or even worse, runs or sags, where the gun changes directions. In situations such as this, it helps to release the trigger a bit sooner than you would on a flat surface, feathering the finish into the area where perpendicular passes may overlap. This may take some practice at first, but as you become

**On flat surfaces like door panels or tabletops, begin by spraying, or 'banding' the four edges first (left). Spray the horizontal surface next (right), working from front to back, toward the exhaust fan.**

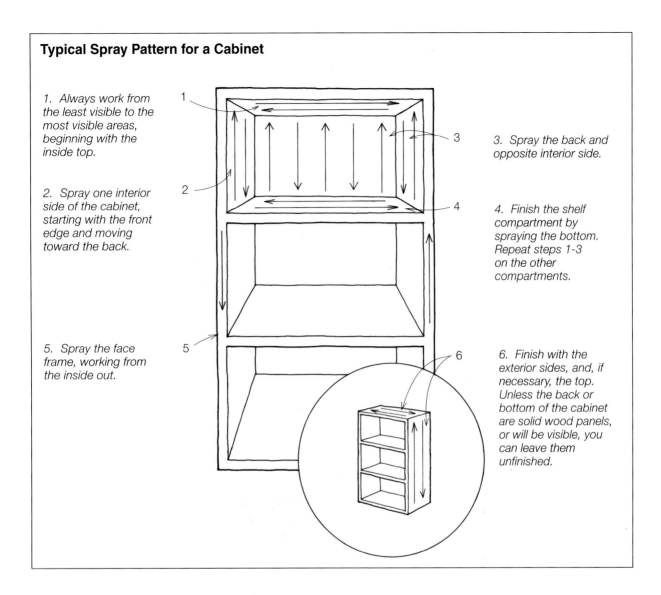

**Typical Spray Pattern for a Cabinet**

*1. Always work from the least visible to the most visible areas, beginning with the inside top.*

*2. Spray one interior side of the cabinet, starting with the front edge and moving toward the back.*

*3. Spray the back and opposite interior side.*

*4. Finish the shelf compartment by spraying the bottom. Repeat steps 1-3 on the other compartments.*

*5. Spray the face frame, working from the inside out.*

*6. Finish with the exterior sides, and, if necessary, the top. Unless the back or bottom of the cabinet are solid wood panels, or will be visible, you can leave them unfinished.*

more familiar with your spray equipment, you will develop a feel for how the gun responds and will become more adept at controlling where and how heavily the finish material is applied. I usually leave the backs and bottoms of cabinets unfinished, unless they are solid wood panels or will be visible. That not only saves labor and material, but also makes the wet cabinet easier to move.

## Production spraying

The key to production spraying lies in how efficiently multiple pieces can be moved through the spray booth. Be creative, and you will discover your own shortcuts. Here are three of mine. To spray pieces of similar size or length, I use trays on baker's racks like the one pictured

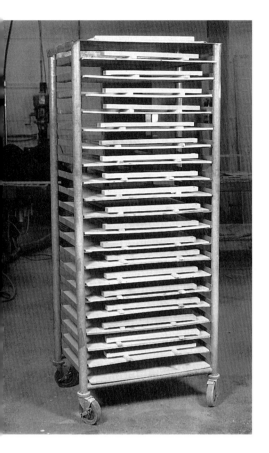

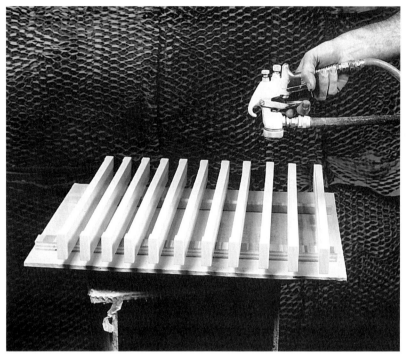

**Handling and moving large numbers of small pieces can be a problem in production spraying. At left, a baker's rack supports shelf edging on trays. A fully loaded tray (above) can easily be removed from the rack, sprayed and set back to dry.**

in the photo above left. A fully loaded tray (see the photo above right) can be removed from the rack; all the items on it can be sprayed at one time, and the tray can be set back on the rack to dry.

Another useful trick for production work, especially for long, slender items like balusters or baseball bats, is to hang the work. Pieces with hooks or staples in one end can be suspended on a wire or clothesline and brought into the booth to be sprayed (see the photo at left on the facing page). Then the finished pieces can be moved to another area to dry. This way the workpieces are easy to handle, and all sides can be sprayed at one time.

The third tip will help you spray small or light objects, which the air from a spray gun tends to blow all over the place. One way to prevent this is to lay the pieces over a piece of screen or hardware cloth (see the photo at right on the facing page). The air from the gun passes by the piece being sprayed and through the screen. The air that hits the target covers it with finish, pinning it in place.

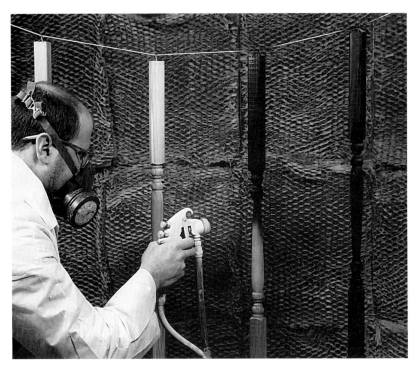

Pieces with hooks or staples in one end can be suspended on a wire or clothesline, brought into the booth to be sprayed and then hung in a separate area to dry. This way all sides can be sprayed at one time.

To spray small or light objects, lay them on a screen or piece of hardware cloth. That way, the air from the gun won't move them around.

Combining all of the variables that go into setting up and spraying a finish may seem a bit overwhelming at first. However, with a little time and practice, the entire process will become second nature, and you will be able to spray a high-quality finish with far less time and effort than you could ever achieve with a brush.

## Troubleshooting

No matter how skilled and careful you are, you are bound to experience some problems while spraying. Most likely, the trouble stems from one of four things: There is something wrong with the equipment, your technique, the way your material has been prepared or the weather. The chart on pp. 152-157 lists common problems that may occur when using different equipment and materials. The causes of most of these are easy to spot and simple to fix. Changing the weather isn't so easy, but as long as you are aware of the potential effects weather may have on your spraying, even problems caused by nature can be overcome.

# CHAPTER 5

# Coloring the Wood

I'm willing to bet that when most people think of spray finishing, they envision laying down multiple coats of clear finish over a stain that has been applied with brushes and rags. However, one of the advantages of owning spray guns is that they can also be used to spray dyes, stains, paints and pigmented lacquers effectively on nearly any surface. The color goes on faster, and it is easier to control where the finish material lands and how thick each coat is.

Applying stain with a rag is a fairly quick process and does not take a lot of skill; however, staining a large project usually involves a great deal of wiping and rubbing and can be quite messy. Using a brush is one method, but if you have ever tried to brush a coat of stain on a large wall unit or set of cabinets, you know how long it can take.

When I first started spray finishing I never considered using my gun to apply stains. My father taught me that stains were applied with rags and elbow grease, and I saw no reason to change. I continued to stain my work the way I always had, saving my spray equipment for the more important task of applying the top coat.

One day a friend of mine, who happens to be in the commercial furniture business, asked me if I would be interested in finishing some dressing-room stools that were headed for a large department store. I was happy to take on the work, until I realized what was involved. Wiping stain on the legs and stretchers of a few stools would be easy,

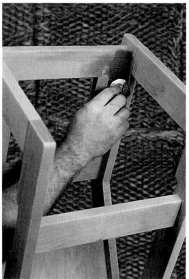

Wiping stains or dyes in tight corners is a real chore. Spray equipment makes short work of the same job by applying a consistent coat of color, even in hard-to-reach places.

but performing the same procedure on dozens would be something else. If I hoped to come up with a realistic price for finishing the stools, I would have to think of a way to apply the stain quickly and consistently on multiple pieces. Needless to say, I rethought my attitude toward using spray equipment for applying stain, and to this day I'm glad that I did.

What's nice about spraying stain is that the technique isn't very difficult. The mechanics are the same as for spraying any other type of finish. So long as you have the right equipment and material and the wood has been prepared properly, very little can go wrong. However, not all stains are a joy to apply. Some types of stains work well with spray equipment, while others are better left to brushes and rags. Consequently, before setting up a finishing schedule you must first decide what type of stain to use and how best to apply it.

# Dye stains

Dye stains, most commonly referred to as aniline dyes, consist of a powder that is dissolved in a solvent to make a mixture that is absorbed deeply into the fibers of the wood. Dyes are transparent (unlike pigmented stains) and add color to wood without hiding its grain or figure. Dye powders are mixed in either water, alcohol or oil. The type you use depends on the size and configuration of the piece being finished, as well as the application method. In general, alcohol- and oil-soluble dyes dry too quickly to be used on big projects, so they are often relegated to specialty applications, including touch-up and repair work. Water-soluble dyes take longer to dry, giving you more time to coat and wipe (if necessary) larger surfaces. Water-soluble dyes are inexpensive, safe and easy to use, and relatively resistant to fading. For these reasons they are the most popular and easiest to spray of the three.

**With dyes, the depth of color is determined by the amount of powder dissolved in the appropriate solvent and by the number of coats applied.**

The only problem with water-soluble dyes is that the water in the solution raises the grain of even the most carefully sanded wood. This means you must add a step to the sanding process, either wet-sanding before spraying, or sanding off the raised grain after the dye is dry.

In an effort to combat the problem of raised grain, manufacturers have dissolved water-soluble dyes in a mixture of solvents, including alcohol and lacquer thinner, to create non-grain-raising, or NGR, dyes, which exhibit the same properties as their water-soluble counterparts while minimizing the amount of raised grain. NGR dyes are sold premixed and can be used straight or thinned with alcohol or lacquer thinner. They can be tinted with powders, mixed with other compatible dyes and used to add color to nearly any finish material. (For more on NGR dyes, see pp. 129-132.)

About the only drawback to NGR dyes is that they are more costly and more toxic than water-soluble powders. And even though they greatly reduce grain raising, they do not eliminate it entirely. As a result, the use of NGR dyes will also require some extra sanding.

I keep a supply of both water-soluble powders and premixed NGR dyes in my shop. On any project I may use one or the other exclusively, or I may create my own colors by mixing combinations of the two.

**Preparing dye stains**
Water-soluble dyes are nice because you mix them yourself, which gives you better control over the final color. The higher the ratio of powder to water, the deeper the color will be. As a starting point, test the manufacturer's recommended mixing ratio, usually around 1 oz. powder to 1 qt. water. If the color is too dark, dilute it with more water. If it is too light, add more powder. I like to mix the dyes a shade lighter in solution and then control the final color by manipulating the thickness and number of coats I apply. The beauty of a water-soluble dye is that if you don't get the color right you can dilute it even after it has been applied by wiping the surface of the wood with water. And if you realize after you are done that the color is completely wrong, you can usually remove it by scrubbing it off with bleach.

Mixing your own dyes is not very complicated. All you need is a glass or plastic container and some warm water. (Though I have often mixed powders in cold water with no ill effects, warm water seems to work better. If you use cold water, the powder will take longer to dis-

**Mix dyes in glass or plastic containers, and always add the powder to the solvent a little at a time until it dissolves.**

solve and will require more stirring.) Add the powder to the solvent a little at a time, until it fully dissolves. I try to mix dyes at least a day before they are needed so that the powder has plenty of time to dissolve, but in a pinch I have used dyes shortly after mixing. To ensure consistency in color and absorption, be sure that the solution comes to room temperature before you use it.

I am probably not as particular about how I mix dyes as I should be, and purists might cringe at my techniques. Because tap water contains minerals that could alter the color of the dye, distilled water is the recommended solvent. However, I never seem to have any distilled water, so I use plain tap water. Also, because the concentration of dyes varies according to weight, not volume, you should use an accurate scale for mixing your own colors. But a good-quality scale that can measure tiny amounts of powder can be expensive and is probably not standard equipment in the average woodworking shop. (Wouldn't you rather spend that money on a new router? I know I would.) Lacking a scale, I mix dyes the way a good chef prepares a meal, adding a pinch of this and a dash of that until I have the right mix. I use ordinary measuring spoons and keep track of the quantity in an attempt to come up with a formula that can be recreated at a

If a dye powder does not dissolve fully, small clumps may form that could mar the finish or clog your spray gun. You can eliminate the risk by straining dyes before you spray them.

later date. Although this trial-and-error approach may not be the most accurate way to mix dyes, I have always been able to match colors from one batch to the next with no noticeable differences.

If a dye powder is not mixed thoroughly and does not dissolve completely, small clumps may form in the solution (see the photo above). These will show up as dark spots on the surface being sprayed or could even clog your spray equipment. For this reason it is always a good idea to strain dyes before spraying (for more on straining, see pp. 74-75).

## Preparing the surface

As with all finishing, the key to success is proper preparation. Because dyes color wood fibers evenly (as opposed to pigmented stains, which lodge in open pores and scratches, highlighting imperfections), sanding is not as critical. Don't get me wrong—I'm not advocating skipping grits or doing a lousy sanding job. I'm simply saying that if a blemish or sanding scratch is missed, it will not be as noticeable under a dye. Obviously, the better the wood is prepared, the better the finish will be. What's important is to maintain an even scratch pattern over the entire piece.

Because of the grain-raising characteristics of water-soluble dyes, an extra round of sanding must be planned for in the finishing schedule. There are two ways to deal with the problem. First, you may raise the wood grain yourself prior to applying the dye. I do this by wetting the surface of the wood with a damp rag or plastic spray bottle filled with water, then let the surface dry completely before sanding off the raised grain with 220-grit paper. Some people insist the wood must dry overnight before sanding, but I think this is silly. How long I wait depends on temperature and humidity, and may be as little as 15 min. to as much as a few hours. Water-soluble dyes are dry enough to sand and recoat in a matter of an hour or two, so why should you have to wait longer when plain water is applied? As soon as the wood looks and feels dry and the fibers are stiff, I begin sanding. If you have been careful in your preparation and sanding, you should be able to apply the dye without having to worry about any additional grain raising.

Second, you can use a coat of dye, rather than water, to raise the grain. Sand the wood as usual, stopping at 180 grit. Next, spray a light coat of dye over the entire piece. This not only raises the grain, but also begins the coloring process. After an hour or so the dye should be dry enough for sanding with 220 grit. If the raised grain is especially rough or difficult to sand, try applying a thinned coat of sealer or a 1-lb. cut of shellac after the first coat of dye has dried. This stiffens the raised wood fibers, making them easier to sand.

## Spraying dyes

Dyes are very forgiving and easy to work with. In fact, they are so simple to spray and give such good results that in my shop the only way I will consider using something other than a water-soluble or NGR dye is if a customer specifically requests a different treatment. Even then, I usually go out of my way to find a dye that matches the customer's color request.

Because the dye completely dissolves in the solvent, the liquid you are spraying is little more than water. As a result, you will have better control over the rate of application if you downsize your fluid tip; for HVLP, I'd use something in the .035-in. to .045-in. range. Because the dye is absorbed into the wood and doesn't sit on the surface the way paint or pigmented stains do, it makes little difference what size air cap you use. The flow rate can be controlled by the fluid-adjustment knob to prevent the dye from going on too heavily. So long as the material is being properly atomized, you should get good results. In fact, I often spray dye stains with the same tip and air cap that I plan to use for the top coat. This not only eliminates the need to change setups, but it helps simplify the cleaning process.

**When applying one heavy coat of dye, it helps to spray a light mist of water over the surface being finished a few minutes before applying the dye. The water 'primes' the wood so it will absorb the dye better.**

Whether you spray thick or thin coats of dye is a matter of personal preference. Extremely light coats mean more applications, lengthening the finishing process. On the other hand, spraying too much dye on an area may cause it to run, leaving steaks or drips that show up as dark, uneven patches in an otherwise uniform coating of color. If you apply a heavy coat, all of the dye may not be absorbed into the wood. In this case, you will have to wipe off the entire piece with a clean rag shortly after spraying. If you plan on coloring the wood in one step by applying a single, heavy coat of dye, lightly mist the surface with a plastic spray bottle and some clean water a few minutes before spraying (see the photo above). The water acts as a primer, softening the wood pores and fibers so they can better absorb the dye.

When spraying a single piece, I generally like to apply the dye in one heavy coat, using a rag to wipe off the excess and even out the color. But when I have a lot of spraying to do, I apply two light coats. I have found that not having to wipe each piece after it has been sprayed speeds up the finishing process. Having to stop and wipe each piece not only interrupts the flow of spraying, but also leaves me with damp, messy rags that end up smearing dye on my hands, clothes and the outside of the gun. For a typical spray schedule for water-based dye, see pp. 158-159.

Although careful control of the flow rate and application of the dye should eliminate the need for wiping after each coat, it is a good idea to have a clean rag on hand to spot-wipe any drips or runs that may occur, especially in areas where the spray patterns overlap.

## Pigmented stains

Unlike dyes, which are transparent and are absorbed into the wood, pigmented stains contain solid particles of color that sit on the surface, lodging in any crevices large enough to hold them, such as pores and sanding scratches. The pigments in these types of stains are opaque and tend to obscure the grain and figure of wood. However, pigmented stains are commonly used in small and amateur shops for several reasons. They are readily available in most paint and hardware stores and come premixed in small and large containers, so they are relatively foolproof, and a certain level of consistency is guaranteed from one can to the next. Also, applying pigmented stains doesn't require special equipment. Simply brush or wipe on a heavy coat, let it dry for a few minutes and wipe off the excess. What could be easier?

The only reason I can imagine for spraying pigmented stains would be if you are working with many pieces and want to speed up the application process. In fact, the only time I ever sprayed a pigmented stain was when I had to finish the top and four sides of 2,000 small cherry blocks. The four edges of the blocks had a routed profile, and it was important that no stain get on the bottom face. I realized that wiping the stain on that many pieces by hand would be tiring and take forever. By laying the blocks out on trays I was able to spray a coat of stain on the sides and tops of all 2,000 pieces in just a few hours. Of course, each block still had to be wiped by hand, which took up the rest of the day. But there is no doubt that applying the stain with a spray gun significantly reduced the overall time required to do the job.

There is one very good reason to avoid spraying pigmented stains: The particles of pigment are relatively large and abrasive and may, over time, destroy the tip of your gun. It is not entirely an exaggeration to say that running pigmented stain through a precisely machined fluid tip will have the same results as spraying a mixture containing sand.

All things considered, I advise you not to use your spray equipment to apply pigmented stains. However, if you decide you must spray a pigmented stain, there are a few things to know.

## Preparing pigmented stains

Pigmented stains are ready to use right out of the can, but you have to make certain the stain is thoroughly mixed and strained. Leaving a big clump of coagulated pigment in the bottom of the can may lighten the color of the stain. Any lumps in the stain are almost sure to find their way into your spray equipment and will quickly plug up an otherwise clean gun.

## Preparing the surface

Because a pigmented stain lodges in the pores of the wood, surface preparation of the item to be sprayed is more critical than when using dyes. Pigmented stains tend to highlight surface imperfections, such as scratches or swirl marks left by a random-orbit sander, so it is important that the wood be as clean and smooth as possible. For this reason I usually sand my projects to 220 grit before applying any stain. If I plan on using a water-based top coat I will raise the grain before this final sanding by spraying or wiping on a light coat of water.

## Spraying pigmented stains

A pigmented stain is applied with a spray gun and then wiped off, just as it would be if applied with a brush or rag: Flood the surface of the wood with stain, let it sit for a few minutes and wipe off what is left. Because of the size of the pigment particles, you should use a larger fluid tip than you would for spraying dyes. In fact, because it is important to get a heavy, even coat over the entire surface, it is better to use a needle/tip combination that is too large, rather than too small. On the one occasion that I used pigmented stain, I got good results using a .051-in. fluid tip. Don't worry about drips or runs—they will be wiped off before they have a chance to dry.

Spraying pigmented stains is a relatively messy job, and getting the gun clean afterwards will require plenty of mineral spirits and patience. With most finish materials, any overspray or mess that is not cleaned up immediately will dry rather quickly. Pigmented stain, unfortunately, stays sticky for a long time, so it is important not only to get the inside of the gun clean, but also to remove the stain from the outside of the gun and the surrounding area as well.

## Gel stain

Gel stain, sometimes referred to as a wiping stain, is thick, pigmented material that is more like a paste than a liquid. This type of stain does not penetrate very deeply, has little or no ability to flow and is designed to stay where you put it. Applying it with a spray gun would be a waste of time, and I can't see why anyone would even want to try. The stain would require so much thinning that the whole purpose of using it would be defeated. Although spray guns are extremely versatile, there are some materials that just aren't suitable for spraying.

## Paint

If you own a spray gun, at some point you will probably use it to spray paint, especially if your equipment is portable. Given a choice, would you like to spend all day painting the shutters on your house with a brush? Or would you rather finish the job in a few hours using a spray gun? There is no doubt that spray equipment makes short work of painting large surfaces, such as the sides of a house, as well as small, intricate items such as balusters. The paint goes on quickly and smoothly, with no brush marks.

Professional painters often use airless equipment to apply paint to walls, ceilings and trim. The material is propelled through the tip of the gun at high pressures and covers large areas in no time. But while the quality of the finish is fine for the side of a house, it may look less attractive on a piece of furniture. In fact, several painters I know have two spray systems. They use airless for everyday projects and HVLP equipment for finer work.

**An air-cap test kit measures the pressure at the tip of the gun when the trigger is pulled.**

Achieving a furniture-quality finish with paint and an air-powered spray gun is not easy, especially if you don't have the right equipment. Achieving a perfectly smooth finish with latex paint is virtually impossible. No matter what equipment you use and how you prepare the material, the surface of the finish will almost always have a slight texture. The problem is worse if your spray gun does not have enough power to atomize the paint completely. If you are spraying latex, you will need a minimum of 5 psi at the tip of the gun to achieve good atomization. One way to check the pressure at the tip of your gun is by using an air-cap test kit (see the photo at left). The kit, which is offered by most manufacturers of good-quality spray equipment, contains an air cap and dial that mount to the head of the gun. As air is triggered through the cap, the dial reads the pressure in pounds per square inch.

Many manufacturers claim that their turbine-driven systems can spray most materials, including latex paint. While it is true that the guns will spray the paint, the results are often disappointing. Turbines with less than three stages are not capable of delivering enough air pressure to the tip of the gun, so chances are if you have a one- or two-stage turbine you are guaranteed to be frustrated with the performance of your equipment when you try to spray paint. This doesn't mean that you will never be able to spray a decent painted finish on a piece of fine furniture. It does mean that you need to do more work and more preparation when using paint than when using other materials.

## Turbines, fluid tips and air caps for spraying paint

If you plan to use your spray gun to apply paint to furniture, it is important to size the equipment accordingly. If you have a large compressor this is not a problem. If you are using a turbine as your air source it must be a minimum of three stages, or you will not be able to achieve good atomization. In fact, if you are looking to buy a turbine and know you will be spraying a lot of paint, it may make sense to get a unit with five or seven stages. Of course, these can get expensive, so you must consider carefully how much paint you will be spraying. In most cases you should be able to get by with a three-stage unit.

Because paints are relatively thick materials, you must size your fluid tip accordingly. When spraying paint I usually use something around a .055-in. fluid tip, and I step the air cap down one size from what I would normally use. The higher-velocity air coming from a smaller cap helps atomize the paint better and reduces the chances of severe orange peel or mottled texturing.

## Preparing the paint

Probably the most important factor in the success of your paint job will be how well you prepare the paint for spraying. Paint is thicker than most materials you would normally spray, and, depending on your equipment, it will probably need to be thinned. Thinning paint for spraying is more difficult than thinning other materials. If you don't use enough thinner, the paint may not atomize and flow together properly, and, in some cases, may not spray from the gun at all. If you use too much thinner, the paint may run, sag and drip. Excessive thinning may also slow down the drying time of paint (especially oil-based paint) and may even cause the paint to lose its color and ability to hide the underlying wood.

When spraying paint I always try to use as little thinner as possible to get the right spray consistency. I do this by testing undiluted paint on a piece of paper or cardboard, then adding small amounts of thinner to the material container until good atomization is achieved. If I plan on using more than a quart of paint, I thin the rest of the paint right in the can. Thinning a large batch of material all at once not only speeds up the spraying process, but also helps the paint flow through the strainer more quickly each time you stop to refill the cup.

Even if your paint is properly thinned and you have good spray equipment, you may still have trouble achieving a smooth coat that flows together evenly. If so, you may want to include a small amount of flow-out additive designed specifically for running paint through spray equipment. Your local paint store should have a selection of additives for both latex and oil-based paint. Don't mistake these products for thinners. Although they seem to lighten the paint, helping it move through the gun better, they are actually designed to improve the way the material flows together on the surface being sprayed. Follow the instructions on the can for good results.

**Preparing the surface**

Because paint calls attention to imperfections, your preparation of the surface is of the utmost importance. Unlike clear finishes, which build layers that tend to hide small surface imperfections, painted finishes actually highlight areas that have been poorly scraped, sanded or filled. Whereas a small nail hole may be barely noticeable after a coat of dye and two or three coats of clear varnish, it will look like a giant crater under a few layers of opaque finish. It usually takes more time and care to prepare a piece for spray-painting than it does for staining. This is especially true if you are using a high-gloss finish, which highlights imperfections and rough spots even more.

Before any paint goes on the piece, the surface must be absolutely smooth. Obtaining this kind of surface involves sanding, filling and priming the piece, then resanding it. The first coat of primer usually highlights defects missed during the initial sanding and filling. These imperfections must then be refilled and resanded. A second and, if necessary, a third coat of primer must then be applied and sanded smooth. Once the entire surface of the piece is perfectly smooth and free of defects, the color coats can be applied.

**Spraying paint**

The mechanics of spraying a painted finish are the same as for spraying any other material. If you are using a light color over a white primer, you may need only one coat. Darker colors will require two coats or more. When working with dark colors it helps to tint the primer before you apply it. Some black pigment in white primer will give you a shade of gray that is easier to cover than white.

On most of my painted projects I am able to achieve a good finish with two coats of primer and one or two coats of color. Occasionally, if I want to add more depth to the surface, I will spray on a couple of coats of clear finish over the color coats. This provides added protection to the painted surface and gives me better control over the final gloss.

## Latex vs. oil

Should you spray latex or oil-based paint on your project? The choice depends on several factors. First, the type of equipment you have may limit your ability to spray heavy-bodied latex paints successfully. If you have a one- or two-stage turbine you will probably have difficulty atomizing the paint fine enough to create a smooth coat. You can try to overcome this problem by using a lot of thinner, but that will make spraying the paint difficult and frustrating.

Second, when you choose the paint, you must consider the quality your project demands. If, for example, you are spraying an exterior porch or shutters, latex paint is a good choice. The finish may not be perfectly smooth and free of orange peel, but who is going to notice?

The finish on a finely crafted piece of furniture is different. Here, a flawed finish will be more noticeable, and it will also make an otherwise perfect piece look rough and unprofessional. If you are having trouble getting a furniture-quality finish with latex paint, you may have to switch to oil-based products. Oil-based paint is easier to thin and spray than latex, and it usually gives better results. Oil-based paints tend to build faster and take on a much higher gloss than latex. Because oil-based paint takes longer to dry, it has more time to flow together over the surface of the wood. Orange peel and textured or mottled surfaces, which are hard to avoid with latex, become less of a problem when spraying oil-based paints.

That is not to say that oil-based paints are foolproof. In fact, the factors that make them an attractive alternative to latex paint are the same factors that work against them. The long drying time may limit surface texturing, but it creates different problems. It takes longer to finish a project because it takes longer for each coat to dry. I have sprayed two, or even three coats of latex paint on the same piece in one day. A coat of oil-based paint must dry at least overnight, and sometimes even longer, before another coat can be sprayed over it.

The longer drying time gives dust a greater chance to settle on the finish, which means you must have a clean spray area and a good place to store the project while it is drying. Pieces that require finishing on all sides will take even longer to complete, since you have to wait for one side to dry before flipping them over to spray the other. Another drawback to using oil-based paint is that cleanup leaves you with a fair amount of mineral spirits, which must be properly stored and discarded.

## Pigmented lacquer

As you have probably concluded by now, I'm not enthusiastic about using spray guns and paint to color wood. Latex does not give the results I need, and oil-based paint takes too long to dry. I have no problem spraying paint on the outside of my house, but I avoid doing it in my shop.

Of course, not all furniture projects are stained and covered with clear top coats. Many of my customers want their cabinets, vanities and wall units to have an opaque, or "painted," finish. In the past, I would occasionally use paint to finish some of these pieces, especially if the

**As a substitute for paint, you can mix your own colors by combining small amounts of universal tints with white lacquer.**

customer requested a specific brand or type, but I was never happy with the finish and would always regret my choice of materials. A few years ago, in an effort to avoid the struggles and problems associated with spraying paint, I began to finish all of my "painted" pieces with opaque lacquers that can be tinted to match any color imaginable.

Colored or tinted lacquers offer several advantages over paint. They are easier to spray and clean up, they dry faster, and they are easier to sand and repair. These pigmented lacquers need little or no thinning and, best of all, give top-quality, consistent results appropriate for the finest pieces of furniture.

Of course, there is one catch—in most cases, you must mix the color yourself. Some manufacturers offer opaque lacquers in a variety of pre-mixed colors. These are great if you are able to use one of the colors they happen to have. Unfortunately, premixed lacquers are usually limited to basic colors like red, green and blue, which won't do you much good when you're trying to match taupe.

Tinting and mixing your own colored lacquers may sound scary at first, but it is actually quite easy. You need only three things: a sample of the color you are trying to match, a good paint store with a computer and a paper cup. The paint store's computerized color-matching system can analyze the sample, breaking it down into the various pigments that make up that color. Once you know the colors and amounts of pigment needed, you can, using a white base, mix an opaque lacquer that is the same color as your sample.

Although the sales clerks are usually confused at first, I have always found that once I explain what I am doing they are more than willing to give me (for a few dollars, of course) the exact mix of pigments I need. I always bring my own cup and am sure to specify whether I need enough tint for 1 gal. or 5 gal. of lacquer.

Getting the correct mix of tints is even easier if you are trying to match a specific brand and color of paint. A store that carries that brand will have the mixing formula in a book and can give you the right pigments without needing a sample or a computer.

Naturally, tinting lacquers is not always as easy as I've just made it sound. Occasionally you may be called upon to match a paint that is "batch mixed." Batch-mixed paints are usually part of a standard line of colors offered by the manufacturer and come premixed directly from the factory. Because they are produced in large quantities, there is no formula for mixing a quart or gallon. In this case you will definitely need the help of the paint store's computer to approximate the right formula.

A potential problem with using the methods described above is the accuracy of the computer that analyzes your color sample. Although I have found that in most cases the computer-generated formulas are fairly close matches, occasionally they have been way off. Usually the colors of the necessary pigments are right, but the amounts are wrong. Sometimes you have to play around with the mix yourself until you get a satisfactory match.

The color of the lacquer base you use may have an impact on how accurate your match is, too, especially when working with lighter colors and variations of white. I learned the hard way that there is no such thing as a standard white. One manufacturer's white may have a yellow undertone, while another brand may look blue. If you are using a white lacquer to match white, or a variation thereof, you may have to adjust the tinting formula to compensate for the base lacquer's inherent shading. Some lacquer manufacturers offer a variety of bases designed specifically for mixing custom colors, which makes the process somewhat easier.

**Universal tints come in a variety of colors and sizes ranging from one-ounce tubes to quart cans.**

Finally, as with all finishing materials, you should be sure the pigments you are using are compatible with the lacquer base. I generally use what are known as universal tints. Available from most paint and art supply stores, they come in containers from 1-oz. tubes to 1-qt. cans, and are compatible with all water-based products and most solvent-based materials. However, not all tints will work with nitrocellulose lacquers. You should always check for compatibility first by mixing a small amount of lacquer and tint in a separate container. It won't take more than a few seconds to discover if the tints will work with your lacquer. The wrong type of tint will immediately break apart into small, sandlike particles that get thrown to the sides of the can.

Despite the potential for slight variations in color, I have found that getting a cup of the appropriate pigments from the paint store and mixing it in a can of white lacquer yields results acceptable to most people. I also keep an assortment of pigments and some measuring spoons on hand for those occasions when I am trying to match an odd color or need a better match than the paint store gave me. Although there are some basic rules for mixing color, it is largely a matter of trial and error that gets easier with experience. If you do a lot of specialty finishes and mix your own colors, you will develop a feel for what works.

### Preparing the surface

Pigmented lacquer, like paint, requires a surface that is absolutely smooth and defect free. Sand, fill, prime and resand, then, if necessary, apply an additional coat or two of primer. The color coat should not be sprayed until the underlying surface is as smooth as possible. In fact, it will usually take a lot longer to prepare the object being finished for the color coats than it will to apply them.

### Spraying pigmented lacquer

Pigmented lacquer should be sprayed in the same way as paint (see pp. 100-103). Because lacquer dries much faster than paint, several coats can usually be applied in only one day. For a typical spray schedule for pigmented lacquer, see p. 161.

# CHAPTER 6

# Working with Top Coats

Whether you color your projects with dye, stain or pigmented lacquers or decide to let the natural wood show through, you will want to protect the surface with some type of clear top coating—lacquer, conversion finish, shellac, water-based finish or oil-based varnish. The finish material you choose will depend on the appearance you are trying to achieve, how much abuse the piece will receive and what your equipment and setup can handle. Knowing the characteristics of the different materials available, how to work with them and how they react with spray equipment will make your choice easier.

## Lacquer

It is no coincidence that industrial lacquers and spray equipment came of age at about the same time. In fact, you could say they were made for each other.

Nitrocellulose lacquer would probably win the award for everybody's favorite material for spraying for several reasons. It is easy to handle and spray. It forms an exceptionally clear film, builds up quickly in just a few coats and allows you to create an illusion of great depth. It is easy to repair and rub out, and it dries fast. Although I avoid solvent-based finishes in my shop, I make an occasional exception with lacquer. There is simply no substitute for lacquer on large cabinet jobs that have to be completed in a hurry and on a budget.

**Since different lacquers have different chemical properties, it is important to use the right thinner for the product you are spraying.**

Lacquer is not fussy to thin. So long as you use the right thinner, you can add as little or as much to the lacquer as you want without having any dramatic negative effects on the finish. However, using the wrong thinner can lead to problems. The chemical composition of lacquer thinner determines how fast solvents evaporate. Using the wrong thinner may cause the lacquer to appear cloudy or dull, or make the surface being sprayed look as if it has been dusted with little specks of lint or cotton (a condition called "cotton blush"). Lacquer manufacturers usually recommend a specific type of thinner for their products. The best way to avoid problems is to stick with what is recommended.

When I spray, I like to maintain as much control as possible over the material and would rather apply several thin layers than one thick coat. As a result, I usually thin the lacquer and for HVLP spraying use a fluid tip somewhere between .035 in. and .045 in. The lacquer film may take longer to build, but it dries so fast I can usually apply several coats in the same day.

As great as it sounds, lacquer has some serious drawbacks. It is toxic and flammable, and prolonged exposure to lacquer fumes may make you dizzy, nauseous and, as my wife will verify, somewhat irritable. If your spray area does not have adequate ventilation, along with appropriate fire and explosion protection (see p. 24), you should not even consider spraying lacquer.

| LACQUER AT A GLANCE | |
| --- | --- |
| **Advantages** | **Disadvantages** |
| It is easy to handle and spray. | It is toxic and flammable. |
| It forms an exceptionally clear film. | It may not meet stringent VOC regulations. |
| It is easy to repair and rub out. | It is prone to fisheye and blush. |
| It dries fast. | It offers relatively low protection against heat, scratches and solvents. |
| It is not problematic to thin. | |

Also, since lacquer offers relatively low protection against heat, solvents and scratches, it may not be the ideal finish in all situations. Lacquer also has a fairly low solids-to-solvent ratio, so less finish ends up on the piece being sprayed and more floats away into the atmosphere. As a result, it takes more coats to build the same thickness of finish you would get with a material that has a higher percentage of solids. The more coats you apply, the more solvent is released into the air. As federal and local governments exert tighter control over air quality, the restrictions against using finishes such as lacquer may eventually become so stringent that using them will become highly restricted. In fact, it wouldn't surprise me if someday soon use of them is legislated out of existence.

Last, a lacquer finish is liable to develop problems if conditions aren't right when it is sprayed. The two most common problems are fisheye and blush.

**Fisheye**

Fisheye, though it can occur with other finish materials, is most often associated with spraying lacquer. Fisheye is characterized by large, circular depressions or holes in the finish (see the photo on the facing page), and is caused by oil or silicone contaminating the surface of the wood or the inside of the spray gun. Fisheye usually appears after you apply the first coat, but sometimes may not show up until you have applied a second or third coat.

There are a few ways to deal with fisheye. If you suspect the contamination is coming from the gun, take it apart and give it a thorough cleaning. Once inside your equipment, silicone is very difficult to remove, so you should always be careful about the lubricants you use on and around your gun.

**Fisheye in a lacquer finish is caused by silicone contamination.**

If the problem originates on the surface of the wood and shows itself while the lacquer is still wet, remove it immediately with some thinner and try cleaning the wood with mineral spirits. If you are confident the problem has been eliminated, start over with a fresh coat of lacquer. To be safe, it may be a good idea to spray a wash coat of a 1-lb. cut of shellac, which will seal in any remaining oil.

If you don't notice the problem until the lacquer is dry, try sanding out the questionable areas until the remaining lacquer is smooth, then recoat them with several very light dustings of lacquer. Once you have several light layers built over the problem spots, lay down a full, wet coat. If all goes well, the last coat will melt the thin layers below but won't go all the way to the contaminant.

There are several products designed to combat fisheye. All these "fisheye eliminators" are silicone additives designed to lower the surface tension of the lacquer so that it is the same as any oil that may be on the surface of the wood. Once you add fisheye eliminator to one coat of lacquer, you must continue to add it to subsequent coats. Most manufacturers will be able to recommend a fisheye eliminator specifically designed for their products.

### Blush

As solvent evaporates from rapidly drying lacquer, it cools the wood and surrounding air enough so that on warm, humid days droplets of water, or dew, may form and get trapped in the lacquer before it is fully dry. Blush appears as a milky white film trapped beneath the surface of the finish. One way to avoid the problem is not to spray on hot, humid days, but that is not always practical, especially if you use your spray gun to make a living. If the humidity is high and you fear the possibility of blush, add some lacquer retarder to the finish before spraying. Lacquer retarder is a slow-drying thinner that allows moisture to escape before the lacquer dries.

If you notice blush after the lacquer is dry, try letting the piece sit for several hours or even a day, to see if the moisture works its way out. If this doesn't work, or if you don't have the time to wait, try dusting on a light coat of straight lacquer retarder. This will redissolve the underlying coat and should allow the moisture to escape.

## Conversion finishes

Conversion finishes, also referred to as crosslinked finishes, are extremely durable, fast-drying finishes that offer excellent protection from heat, solvents and water. They are composed of a combination of resins that react with a catalyst, crosslinking to form a tough finish. There are several different conversion finishes, most of which are used by large furniture factories and would seldom be found in amateur or small professional shops. Two of these finishes, conversion varnish and catalyzed lacquer, occasionally find their way into the finishing rooms of casual woodworkers.

| CONVERSION FINISHES AT A GLANCE | |
|---|---|
| **Advantages** | **Disadvantages** |
| They are easy to handle and spray. | They are toxic and flammable, and emit formaldehyde as they cure. |
| They don't usually require thinning. | They require the addition of a catalyst. |
| They are durable, and build quickly. Only two coats are usually needed. | They have a short working time; you must clean your spray equipment before the finish in it hardens. |
| They dry fast. | They must be sanded carefully, to avoid leaving witness lines. |

Conversion varnish is composed of various resins that react with an acid catalyst, crosslinking together to form a tough, fast-drying film. Catalyzed lacquer is conversion varnish that has nitrocellulose lacquer added to help speed curing. As with conversion varnish, an acid catalyst must be added to the lacquer before it can be sprayed. Precatalyzed lacquers come with the catalyst already added and are often used by small cabinet shops. These finishes work well on pieces that get a lot of wear and abuse, such as bathroom vanities and kitchen cabinets.

Conversion finishes handle, spray and dry almost exactly like nitrocellulose lacquer (see pp. 108-109). The fluid tip, air cap, surface preparation and spraying techniques are the same. Only the material preparations differ. With most conversion varnishes and catalyzed lacquers the use of thinner is not needed and may, in fact, be discouraged. If you must thin, be sure to use the thinner recommended by the manufacturer for the particular product.

Despite the similarities to nitrocellulose lacquer, conversion finishes have their own separate characteristics. Unlike lacquer, which melts, or burns, into the previous coat, conversion finishes form separate layers of film. Therefore, sanding between coats must be performed with greater care. Conversion finishes have a higher solids content than lacquer, so they build faster. With conversion finishes it is easier to apply a thicker coat, which can then be sanded or rubbed out with less chance of cutting through the finish. In fact, if the surface is properly prepared and you do a good job of spraying, two coats of finish are usually all you need.

Despite their ease of use and durability, conversion varnishes and catalyzed lacquer have some serious drawbacks that make them less than ideal for small shop owners. First, you must add the catalyst to the finish, an extra step that leaves room for error. Also, conversion finishes have a relatively short working time and can ruin your spray gun if you don't get it clean before the finish hardens. Finally, conversion finishes are not only highly toxic and flammable, but they emit formaldehyde as they cure. (This is true even of water-based conversion finishes.) If you don't have good ventilation and a proper vapor mask, you should not work with these finishes. Although I do use precatalyzed lacquer on occasion, I generally avoid conversion varnishes and catalyzed lacquers in my shop.

# Shellac

Shellac has acquired the reputation of being old-fashioned—a material well suited for refinishing work, but with no place in a modern shop. This I think overstates the case. Although shellac does not stand up to water, heat and alcohol as well as other finishes, it does some things so well that it is a mistake not to include it in your finishing arsenal.

While it is true that shellac is not the best finish for a tabletop or chair seat, it still makes an attractive choice for pieces that don't get a lot or wear or abuse. I regularly use a 3-lb. cut of shellac, slightly thinned for easier spraying, to coat the interiors of drawer boxes and cabinets (see the photo below). Because shellac is nontoxic when fully cured, it also works well on children's toys and furniture.

Shellac is safe and easy to use, dries amazingly fast, bonds to almost any other finish, and does an exceptional job of sealing in stains, oils, grease and wood resins. Best of all, when it comes to spraying, shellac is virtually foolproof. In fact, it is probably my favorite material.

Unlike most finishes, shellac has a very short shelf life. If the shellac is old it will lose its ability to dry. No matter how long you wait, you will be left with a sticky mess. To avoid this, you can mix your own shellac as needed, or, if you buy it premixed, keep an eye on the date and discard anything more than six months old. One manufacturer guaran-

**Because shellac dries so fast, it's good for sealing and topcoating drawer boxes and cabinet interiors.**

| SHELLAC AT A GLANCE | |
| --- | --- |
| **Advantages** | **Disadvantages** |
| It dries fast and sands easily. | It is extremely flammable. |
| When dewaxed, it bonds to almost any other finish. | It has a short shelf life. |
| It seals in stains, oils, grease and wood resins. | It is not very resistant to water, heat and alcohol damage. |
| It forms a nontoxic film when cured. | |

tees a shelf life of three years and even dates the cans. Although I have no reason to doubt the claim, I have never had a can around for more than a few months, so I can't vouch for it.

If you are unsure of how old your shellac is, place a drop on a piece of wood and let it sit for a few hours. If the shellac is no good, the drop will get sticky or gummy, but it will not fully harden. A good guideline when using shellac is "When in doubt, throw it out."

### Mixing and dewaxing shellac

Shellac can be bought premixed, or you can make your own by combining shellac flakes and denatured alcohol. The amount of shellac flakes in a gallon of alcohol is referred to as the "cut." For example, a can of 5-lb. cut contains a mixture of 5 lb. of shellac flakes for every gallon of alcohol. The cut of shellac that is commonly available at most paint and hardware stores is 3-lb., and that is what I usually have on hand in my shop.

Shellac contains natural wax, which not only clouds its appearance, but limits its ability to bond to many types of finishes. If this wax is not removed, the effectiveness of shellac as a wash or barrier coat between finishes is significantly reduced. You can buy "blonde" shellac (shellac that has been dewaxed), but usually only in large quantities. An easy alternative is to dewax small amounts yourself. Let the can sit for a day or two so the wax has a chance to settle to the bottom of the container (see the photo at right); if you are careful you can simply pour the pure shellac off the top, leaving the wax behind. I usually transfer a gallon can of new shellac into four 1-qt. glass jars and let it settle overnight. The next day I transfer the shellac into a larger container and discard the wax. (Obviously if you are going to use dewaxed shellac you must plan ahead.) I always keep some on hand, and make up new batches before the old ones run out.

**The naturally occurring wax in shellac will eventually settle to the bottom of a can or jar if left undisturbed for a day or two.**

## Shellac as a sealer

Because I use a lot of water-based products in my shop, I am regularly faced with compatibility problems with oil-based stains and finishes. Although the formulations of water-based products have improved greatly over the past several years so that compatibility is less of a problem, I never take a chance. Whenever I am using two materials that may have the slightest chance of a compatibility problem, I spray a wash coat of shellac between them. A 1-lb. cut of dewaxed shellac will seal the first coat, allowing two otherwise incompatible materials to bond.

## Thinning and spraying shellac

Because alcohol is extremely flammable, great care should be taken when spraying shellac. If you don't have the proper ventilation and fixtures, don't try to spray it at all.

### Oil and water do not mix

The first time I saw a water-based product in action was when Bert, my partner at the time, decided to apply it over an oil-based stain. Why he was doing this slips my mind, but I think it had something to do with not wanting the finish to change the color of the stain he had spent two weeks trying to get right. Water-based finishes were new to us, and common sense, combined with a little research, told us there was a potential for problems. Bert spoke to the manufacturer of the stain, who assured him that as long as the stain was allowed to dry long enough, the water-based polyurethane would adhere. Thus encouraged, Bert bravely forged ahead.

After letting the stain dry for over 24 hours (the can said it needed only eight hours before top-coating), Bert sprayed on a nice coat of finish. When he was done I had to admit that the intricately shaped feet of the queen-sized bed were beautiful. After a few rounds of mutual congratulations, we headed home for the night.

The next day I arrived to find Bert hunched over the headboard, hard at work with pads, brushes and scrapers—all implements associated with finish removal. When I asked him what he was doing, he replied rather nonchalantly, "Peeling off the finish, of course." Upon closer inspection I saw firsthand what happens when two incompatible finishes are used together. The water-based polyurethane had bubbled and peeled and was generally trying to get as far away from the solvent-based stain as it could.

Bert did a good job of cleaning up the mess and eventually finished the project to everyone's satisfaction by spraying a barrier coat of dewaxed shellac between the stain and the water-based finish. We learned a simple and valuable lesson. If an oil-based stain is not completely cured (not just dry), getting a good bond with a water-based top coat may be a real problem. To ensure success when working with potentially incompatible materials, allow each coat to dry fully and always apply a barrier coat of appropriate sealer (like dewaxed shellac) between finishes.

That said, shellac is a forgiving material that can be sprayed through any gun with nearly any needle and air cap. I usually use a tip with a .045-in. diameter but have had success with both smaller and larger tips. As with most materials, it is better to spray several light coats rather than one heavy one. Light coats dry faster, and they are also easier to sand. Shellac has a tendency to raise the grain of wood slightly, so it is usually necessary to sand after the first coat. Although a 3-lb. cut can be sprayed straight from the can, it is a good idea to thin the shellac with denatured alcohol. The amount of thinner you add depends on how finely you want the shellac to spray and on what you want the shellac to do. If you are using the shellac as an initial sealer or as a wash coat between two coats of stain or finish, thin it to a 1-lb. cut by adding 2 gal. of alcohol to 1 gal. of a 3-lb. cut. If you are worried that a potential problem may arise because the surface of the wood may contain resin or may be contaminated with wax or oil, don't thin the shellac as much. In this case, something closer to a 2-lb. cut would be appropriate. I often spray a 1-lb. cut of shellac as a sanding sealer over water-soluble dyes. The grain raised by the dye is stiffened by the shellac, which makes sanding easier.

**At left, a 3-lb. cut of shellac; at right, a dewaxed, 1-lb. cut. The difference is clearly apparent.**

Regardless of how much you cut the shellac, it can be very corrosive when it comes into contact with aluminum and will pit the inside of your material cup if left in the gun too long. If you spray a lot of shellac, be sure to clean the gun thoroughly as soon as you are done for the day.

### Blush

About the only problem to watch for when spraying shellac (other than the usual problems associated with spraying) is blush. As with lacquer, blush is caused by moisture that is trapped in the shellac as it dries. The cause could be high humidity or the shellac itself. If the weather seems to be the problem, try letting the shellac dry longer. If the blush does not disappear, sand through and spray again. Sometimes there may be water in the shellac, in which case throw it out and try a new batch.

## Water-based finishes

If you haven't guessed it by now, I'm a big proponent of water-based finishes and could probably write a book devoted to the topic. Water-based finishes have been around for quite a while, but until recently there was not much demand or interest in developing the technology. As a result, with the exception of latex paint, water-based products were relatively scarce and left a great deal to be desired.

**Water-based top coats are versatile, nontoxic and relatively safe to spray.**

However, as air quality became more of an issue in the 1980s, especially in Southern California, government agencies began regulating the amount of volatile organic compounds (VOCs), that finishers could release into the air. In some parts of the country, only products with a high solid-to-solvent ratio comply with some of these strict new standards. As companies that do a lot of finishing began to adapt to changing requirements, they looked to water-based products as a potential solution to their compliance problems. The resulting increase in demand led to advancements in water-based finish technology, and the number of products available has skyrocketed. Today, nearly every manufacturer of finishing materials offers a line of water-based products.

All of this effort on the part of finish manufacturers has led to the present generation of water-based lacquers and urethanes. Although these products are not yet equal to a good varnish or nitrocellulose lacquer in terms of their durability, ease of application and appearance, manufacturers have made great strides in trying to eliminate some of the problems that initially gave the products a bad reputation.

Despite these problems, I have found a few water-based products that are fairly easy to use and give good results. Although there is no question that they can be temperamental to apply and require a bit more work and preparation, I feel the benefits they offer to both the user

| WATER-BASED FINISHES AT A GLANCE | |
|---|---|
| Advantages | Disadvantages |
| They are nonflammable. Because they can't catch fire, they are ideal for people who don't have spray booths. | Water raises wood grain, so surface preparation and sanding are more of an issue. |
| They are nontoxic and emit a relatively low level of solvents. | High humidity can slow drying time from a sprint to a crawl. |
| High solids content means finishes build fast. | Products are extremely sensitive to thinning. |
| They dry fast, and in ideal conditions, can be sanded in less than an hour. | Spray equipment must be stainless steel to prevent corrosion, unless special precautions are taken. |
| They dry clear and are non-yellowing, forming a very hard, scratch-resistant finish. | They are less resistant to heat, solvents and water than a varnish finish. |
| They clean up with water, which further reduces the need for toxic solvents. | |

**A decent-sized window fan or an open window or door is all the ventilation you'll need when spraying water-based finishes. In a larger shop this whole-house fan will do the job.**

and the environment make them worthwhile. Besides, I suspect it is only a matter of time before government regulations mandate their use. I prefer to learn to use a new product at my own pace, rather than being forced to use it because there are no longer any alternatives.

### Equipment

With water-based products, your choice of equipment is more critical than with other types of material. If your equipment is not stainless steel or plastic, it may eventually corrode. One way to prevent this is to be sure that after each use the gun is clean and dry. A prolonged blast of compressed air is one way to dry the gun. If you don't have a compressor, run a few ounces of denatured alcohol through the gun after it has been cleaned.

In addition to having the right kind of spray gun, your air source must be sufficient to atomize water-based products completely. These finishes do not differ greatly in composition and consistency from latex paint (see pp. 100-101). In fact, some of the pigmented lacquer primers I use are as thick as latex. A greater ratio of solids to solvent, combined with a relatively high surface tension, makes water-based products difficult to atomize and less likely to flow out into a smooth film. If your equipment can't deliver enough air pressure to the tip of the gun, you will have trouble achieving a good finish.

**If water-based finish starts to run or drip it is best to wipe it off immediately and respray the entire area.**

## Thinning water-based finishes

If water-based products are tough to atomize and don't flow out very well, why not keep adding thinner until everything works the way it should, you might ask. I have tried this approach and believe me, more thinner is not the solution. In fact, adding thinner to water-based products is probably the worst thing you can do. Too much thinner (and in some cases this means even a small amount) may create more problems than it solves. Because of their high solids content, water-based products are prone to runs, sags and drips. Adding thinner to an already fussy finish will only make it more problematic. Too much thinner reduces the build and can significantly increase the drying time. If you must thin water-based finishes you can use water, but I would recommend checking with the manufacturer first to see if there is a flow-out additive designed specifically for the product.

## The effects of weather

Water-based products are very sensitive to temperature and humidity. If you are spraying on a warm, dry day you will find these products a joy to use. Under ideal conditions they dry to the touch in a matter of minutes and can be sanded and recoated in less than an hour.

However, if the weather gets more humid or colder, you may think you are using an entirely different product. On a rainy day the same finish that dries in 10 minutes under normal conditions may still be wet after an hour. You can forget about sanding for several hours and will be lucky to apply a second coat the same day.

No matter what you do, it is virtually impossible to eliminate the role outside conditions play when you use water-based finishes. If you can control the temperature and humidity in your finishing room, you will be able to minimize most of the problems associated with weather. Although I have no dehumidification equipment in my shop, I have found that a heat lamp, combined with good air movement over the drying pieces, reduces the effects of high humidity and shortens the drying time to tolerable periods.

## Spraying water-based finishes

As long as you have the right equipment and have properly prepared the surface being sprayed and the finish material, the mechanics of spraying water-based lacquers and urethanes are no different from spraying any other material. I generally use a fluid tip of about .050 in. and, with my turbine-driven HVLP system, an air cap one size smaller than usual. I find the smaller air cap breaks the finish into finer particles, thereby reducing the risk of orange peel. With a compressed-air gun I use the same size tip and run the air pressure 5 psi to 10 psi higher than the manufacturer recommends.

There is no denying that spraying water-based finishes requires more care and preparation than spraying their solvent-based counterparts. This doesn't mean it is impossible to get a good finish, but it does take more work. Their annoying habit of raising the grain means an extra sanding step must be inserted into the spray schedule. Wet-sand before applying the stain or finish, or wait until after the first coat of finish has been sprayed—the choice is up to you. But at some point, you will have to sand off the raised grain.

If you are spraying water-based finishes and set the gun down for a minute or two, you'll notice that small drops have a tendency to dry on the fluid tip, restricting the flow of material. When this happens, simply use your fingernail or a toothpick to remove the dried finish.

## Orange peel and other problems

Using a spray gun to apply water-based finishes creates the potential for the same types of problems found with most other materials. In general, the problems associated with spraying water-based products

**Freshly sprayed water-based finishes often look worse than they are. This surface, which appears to have a severe case of orange peel, will level out and become smooth as the finish dries, and the air bubbles will 'pop' out.**

result from three things: too much thinner, applying heavy coats or the weather. Orange peel in particular is a problem (see the sidebar on p. 124) and is usually caused by insufficient atomization pressure. It may also be the result of too much air moving over the freshly sprayed finish or improper application techniques (holding the gun too close or too far away from the target).

The photo above shows exaggerated examples of two characteristics common to water-based finishes. First, the just-sprayed surface shows clearly how water-based products often appear to have severe orange peel while they are wet. As the finish dries, it will level out and become smooth. Second, note the presence of large bubbles, which are caused by air that was trapped in the finish as it was stirred and strained. Usually these will "pop" out of the finish. However, if the coat is sprayed too heavily or there has been a large amount of air mixed into the liquid, tiny bubbles may become trapped in the finish. This is not as much of a problem with opaque finishes as with clear coats. The tiny bubbles, often called microbubbles, may actually cloud the surface with a haze, obscuring the wood or stain underneath.

## A miraculous 'cure' for orange peel

The first time I sprayed a water-based product I was fairly confident of what I was doing. After all, I had been using a brush to apply water-based polyurethane for some time, and spraying, I reasoned, could only make the finish better. I knew that you had to be careful thinning the stuff, so I first tried spraying it straight. As soon as I examined the freshly sprayed test piece I knew I was going to have to add a little thinner. The surface had some of the worst orange peel I had ever seen. I poured an ounce of water into the cup and tried again on a fresh piece. The results were the same. After another ounce of water I still had an amazing amount of orange peel. In went another ounce of water, out came the same horrific orange peel. The test pieces began to pile up on my bench.

The project I was working on had to be finished and installed the next day, and I was running out of time, patience and test pieces. No matter how much thinner I added, the results were the same. Frantic calls to the manufacturers of both my spray equipment and the finish material yielded the same results. My equipment was fine, I was using the proper fluid tip and air cap and there was no reason for the orange peel. The finish manufacturer warned against using too much thinner, but at this point I thought that was the least of my problems.

After my phone calls I discovered that for some reason the orange peel on the last test piece sprayed was almost gone. It was late, and I was behind schedule, so I decided to go ahead and spray the cabinet with the finish I had been thinning and testing for the past two hours.

Once I began spraying I noticed something odd. On horizontal surfaces everything seemed fine, but on the vertical faces, the overthinned finish was running down the sides of the cabinet like water (which is practically all it was at this point). I wiped off the drips and runs and turned down the flow of material until I was able to get an even coating over the entire piece. I cleaned the gun and went home for the night, hoping that if I sprayed another coat early enough the next day I would still be able to deliver the cabinet by the afternoon.

The next morning I was faced with what amounted to an unfinished cabinet. If I looked hard I could see some evidence that a finish had been applied, but it was so thin that it was practically invisible. I had thinned the material so much that all I was really doing was dampening the cabinet with some expensive water.

By this time, I was convinced that water-based products simply could not be sprayed.

Before I grabbed a brush to finish the job, I called my painter friend Bruce, who had talked me into using this polyurethane in the first place. He was surprised that I was having such a problem with orange peel. Once it dries, he assured me, the initial orange peel common to all water-based products disappears. I didn't want to sound stupid, so I grunted my thanks and hung up. Sure enough, when I examined the all-but-forgotten test pieces I was amazed. Except for the very first one, which was straight finish, all the orange peel was gone. How could this be?

I soon discovered what had happened. Because water has such a high surface tension, it does not flow out as easily and quickly as other solvents. As a result, when water-based products are first sprayed they tend to have the lumpy look of orange peel. Over time the finish eventually forms a smooth coat. Depending on your equipment, the material and the weather, this may take minutes or even a few hours.

I learned the hard way that orange peel in a freshly sprayed coat of water-based finish is no reason to panic. Now when I'm not sure if a finish is going on properly, I wait for a sample to dry before reaching for the thinner. (In case you were wondering, once my problem was solved I applied several beautiful coats of finish and delivered the cabinet late in the afternoon—the next day.)

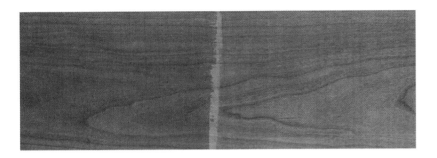

Water-based finishes often make the wood look dull and lifeless. (This is especially on dark woods such as walnut or cherry.) In the example shown here, a coat of nitrocellulose lacquer was sprayed on the left and a coat of clear water-based lacquer on the right.

Another complaint about water-based finishes is that they give the wood a bland, washed-out appearance (see the photo above). While it is true that they dry so clear they don't impart any warmth or color to the wood the way a solvent-based finish does, there are ways around this. Some manufacturers have begun adding a slight amber tint to the product. You can do this yourself by adding a little water-soluble dye powder, universal tint or premixed NGR dye to the finish before spraying it. A very small touch of red or brown dye will go a long way toward creating the look of an oil-based finish.

The fact that water-based finishes dry very clear can be an advantage. Because they are non-yellowing, they are ideal for top-coating lighter-colored woods and pickled finishes and come in handy when you don't want to darken the underlying color.

## Oil-based varnishes

While it is true that any finish that can be brushed on can be run through a spray gun, there are some that should be avoided. Although wiping oils and solvent-based varnishes can be sprayed, I don't know why anyone would want to. They dry very slowly, which not only defeats one of the main reasons for spraying, but also means they leave a sticky residue over your equipment and everything else in the room. If you do have to spray an oil-based varnish, add a generous amount of thinner and spray each coat as lightly as possible. I have sprayed oil-based varnish only once in my life, after which I swore I would never do it again. Some things are better left to brushes.

# CHAPTER 7

# Specialty Applications

A spray gun is no different from any other piece of equipment: As you become more experienced and comfortable using it, you discover tricks and techniques that can expand its limits. Using your spray gun to apply bands of color, spraying the stain and top coat in one shot, and speckling or texturing painted finishes are just a few of the techniques waiting to be mastered. Your equipment can also be used to apply materials you may not normally associate with spraying, such as contact cement.

Following are some examples of the unique finishes that can be achieved with spray equipment. Combining these techniques with imagination and experimentation will allow you to expand the variety and quality of the finishes you spray.

## Shading and toning

Sometimes a freshly sanded piece of wood looks relatively uniform in color, but it may not be. Unfortunately, wild discrepancies often do not show until a coat of stain has been applied. If you are using pigmented stains, blending the various colors together by applying another coat of stain may slightly darken or muddy the appearance of the wood, but it will do little to even out the color variations. In fact, the stain will probably draw attention to whatever irregularity you were trying to hide.

**This cherry board has one coat of water-soluble dye on the right and two coats on the left. Note that the color does not really change, just the tone or depth.**

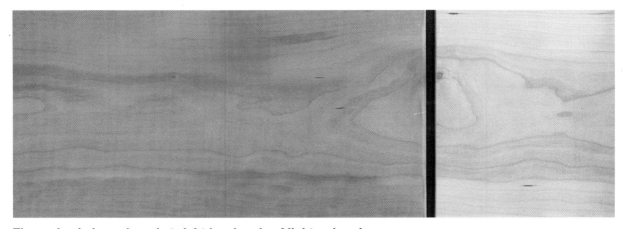

**The undyed cherry board at right has bands of light-colored sapwood along the top and bottom edges. Spraying a very light coat of a cherry-colored water-soluble dye blends the heartwood and sapwood together, as seen at left.**

In situations like this, dye stains and spray equipment come in handy. Because dyes are translucent, they readily lend themselves to "shading," a process in which additional applications of colored finish are selectively layered over previous coats (see the photo at top). Shading is an effective way to mask defects or blend color variations such as sapwood/heartwood in cherry or walnut to make the finish look more even (see the photo above). It can also be used to highlight or draw attention to certain aspects of a piece, such as a particularly striking band of grain. Shading is often used to add layers of color to the edges of cabinets or raised panels, helping frame them while creating an illusion of greater depth, or it can be used to make a new piece look like

The 'sunbursts' on musical instruments consist of several bands of color sprayed in striking patterns. The example above contains six different shades of yellow, orange, red and brown.

**Shading is an effective way to draw attention to certain areas or pieces of wood.**

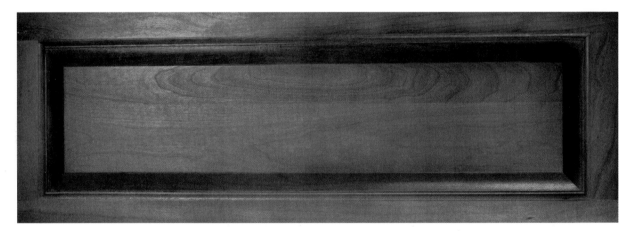

**Shading is commonly used to highlight the edges of raised panels, giving them the illusion of greater depth.**

**Shading moldings helps accent graceful curves or high and low spots and can also be used to create an old or antique look.**

an old or worn antique. Shading is also a common technique used by instrument makers to create dramatic sunburst effects on the backs of guitars and violins.

Like shading, toning involves applying colored coats of finish, only with this technique the material is applied evenly over the entire piece. Toning is used for a number of reasons. In production situations it is a way to combine two finish operations by spraying the color and finish in one shot. It may also be used as one or more coats in a multiple-step finish to change the color of the wood while sealing it, helping create more color and depth in the overall finish.

The procedures for shading and toning are pretty much the same. How much dye or color you add to the finish depends on several factors and is really a matter of experimentation. Begin by mixing a small batch and testing it on a sample. The color can then be adjusted by altering the ratio of dye to clear finish. In general, more dye and less fin-

**This panel was sprayed with one coat of water-soluble dye and clear-coated with a water-based lacquer. The left side was then resprayed with lacquer that had a few ounces of the same dye added. Note how the left side has a deeper, richer color—a good example of toning.**

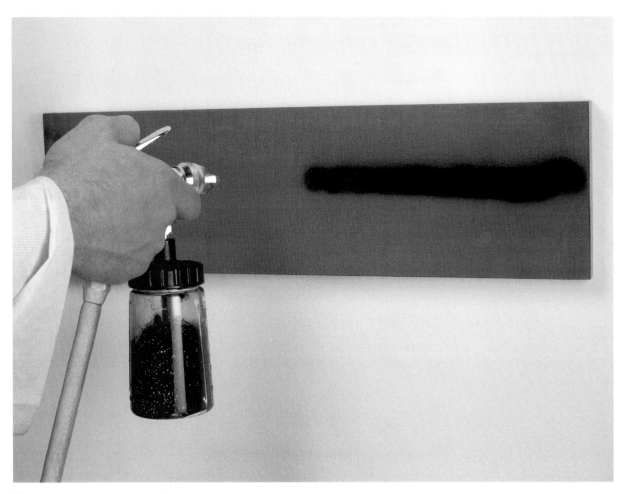

**Touch-up guns are a good investment if you plan on doing a lot of shading. They offer control and pinpoint accuracy that can't be matched by larger equipment.**

ish mean deeper color and slower build. Diluting the clear finish too much may lessen its ability to seal the color, which may then separate or run out of the finish.

When toning a surface, spray the mix as if it were clear, using the same techniques and gun settings. When shading, you need to have complete control over how much material leaves the gun and where it lands. If you do a lot of shading you may want to invest in a small touch-up gun that sprays a fine, accurate mist (see the photo above). Otherwise, try turning the air and fluid regulator knobs on the gun until they are almost completely closed. Quick motions and a light touch, combined with the proper amount of fluid and a small fan pattern, will help you control the shading process.

**When shading, be careful how you mix and apply the tinted finish. Too much dye in the finish or coats that are too thick may cause the color to run, particularly where spray passes overlap, as in the lower right corner of this footstool.**

Although the mechanics for shading and toning are similar to those used to apply any clear finish, there are two potential pitfalls. First, because the finish contains a certain amount of tint or color, it should be initially sprayed in thin coats. If the coating goes on too thick, you may end up with color that is dark in some spots and light in others, a particularly annoying outcome when you spray areas that overlap. Spraying thin coats gives you better control over how much color goes onto the surface. If the color is too light, you can always add more dye to the mix and spray another thin coat.

Second, pay careful attention to your sanding technique. Sanding through a clear finish to bare wood is a situation that, although not desirable, is not usually too hard to fix or disguise. When the color and finish are combined, however, sanding must be done much more carefully. A cut-through shaded or toned coat is more difficult to repair, since adding finish to the trouble spot will actually highlight it by darkening the surrounding area. (Of course this can also work to your advantage in certain cases, especially if you want to give your piece an antique or worn look.)

## Specialty painting

A painter I know makes a fairly good living by specializing in unusual finishing techniques such as sponging and marbleizing, which don't require any special equipment. However, two of the finishes he uses with great success require a spray gun. The first one, called multifleck, is used to give a painted finish a speckled and somewhat textured look (see the top photo on the facing page).

A multifleck finish involves spraying a layer of specially prepared paint over a primed surface. There are several different brands that have the colored specks already mixed in with a tinted base. Before spraying such a finish, the wall or surface must be properly sealed or primed. The speckled paint is then sprayed evenly over the entire area. The size, density and spacing of the flecks of color are controlled by adjusting the fluid flow, atomizing air and speed of application. To get a uniform coating, it is important to keep the gun the same distance from the target and move it at a constant speed. As with any large surface, making a series of two perpendicular passes will help avoid any misses or light spots (see the drawing on p. 85).

If you are spraying a sizable area, such as a wall, you may run into a problem keeping the coating even from one spot to the next. A quick trigger finger and loose wrist should help you feather your passes together while avoiding excessive paint buildup where two sections intersect. You can control the size and density of the color specks by adjusting the air pressure and fluid flow, in combination with how fast you move the gun and how close you hold it to the wall surface.

The second technique, called a spatter finish (see the bottom photo on the facing page), uses mineral spirits sprayed over tacky oil-based paint to create a textured look, while revealing the color of a previously applied base coat. You could use latex paint and water, but because it dries so fast you have to work very quickly. Also, latex products tend to be a bit duller and do not build as fast as oil-based paints, so the results will not be as dramatic.

**Multifleck finishes are popular in high-end homes, and they are used in commercial buildings as well because they do a good job of hiding dirt.**

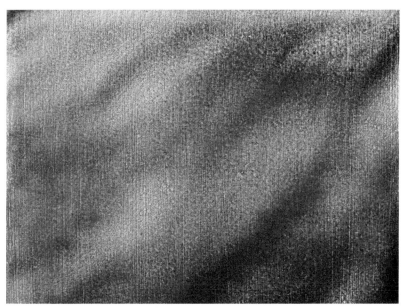

**A spatter finish is created by spraying solvent over a thinned coat of tacky paint. The solvent removes some of the top layer to reveal another coat of color that has been applied underneath. How much of the base coat shows through depends on how fast and heavily the solvent is sprayed.**

Once the wall being painted is fully primed, the next step is to lay down an even base coat. Since this coat will show through the top coat, be sure to select the appropriate color and gloss. Wait until the base coat is completely dry (usually overnight), and then spray an even, full top coat over the entire area. For best results, the top coat should be thinned almost 50%. Thinning the paint not only speeds up the drying process but also helps the base coat show through the final finish more clearly.

Allow the top color coat to set up until it's slightly tacky, then spray a light wash of thinner over the surface. Turn the air in your gun way down so the solvent comes out in relatively large drops. (If you are using a compressor this is easy. If you have a turbine-driven system, a valve can be inserted on the end of the hose that controls the flow of air into the handle of the gun.) As the solvent hits the tacky paint it leaves tiny pockmarks and streaks, allowing the base coat to show through while giving the surface a textured look. How much air you use, how big the drops of solvent are and how densely you spray will determine the final texture of the finish. Be careful not to spray too much thinner, or the paint may begin to run.

## Using spray cans

One day a friend of mine happened by the shop just as I was beginning to spray a coat of finish on a single cabinet door. He looked with some disbelief at the aerosol can of lacquer in my hand and shook his head. "Very professional. Don't you have a spray gun?"

"Of course I do" was my somewhat irritated reply. "But this is cheaper, quicker, easier and gives the same results. Which would you use?"

Aerosol spray cans have always occupied an important spot in my finishing room and always will. Although I use them primarily for touch-up work, they also come in handy on small projects that don't justify the time needed to set up and clean a full-sized spray gun. I regularly use aerosol cans of lacquer to do spot repairs on new cabinets that have been dinged or scratched during installation.

**Many finishes that come in liquid form also come in spray cans.**

**Spray cans are practical for small jobs and touch-up work and give results comparable to larger spray equipment.**

When most people think of spray cans they probably envision paint. Anyone who has ever worked with a can of spray paint is (most likely without realizing it) using the same techniques, motions and skills required for spray guns. In fact, the only difference between using a gun and a can is that with a can there is no mixing, straining or mess to clean up. The spray that comes from a can is usually finer than that from a gun, and cans are easier to control. But because the spray is so light, you often have to apply more coats to get the same build.

Nearly any type of sprayable finish comes in cans. Some lacquer manufacturers offer a complete array of aerosols to match every product in their line. If you have ever had to bring a door or drawer front back to the shop for another coat of finish you know how convenient this can be. I have used spray cans of polyurethane, lacquer, paint, solvents and even spar varnish with great success. For me, the time saved by using spray cans on smaller projects is well worth their relatively high cost.

## Spraying contact cement

If you do a lot of laminate work, either wood or plastic, you know what a chore it is to spread a thick, even layer of contact cement on the surfaces being mated. If you are making only one small countertop or laminating a few pieces of veneer, it is probably not worth the effort of dirtying your spray equipment. However, if you are faced with a big job, you may want to consider using your gun to apply the contact cement.

If you plan on using your gun in this way, be sure the contact cement you buy is designed specifically for spraying. Sprayable contact cements are a bit thinner and less stringy than the brushable types found in most hardware stores and can usually be found at cabinet-supply shops and commercial paint stores.

Although the cement is designed to be sprayed, it is still relatively thick and should not be thinned. I have had success with a fluid tip as small as .051 in. using a water-based glue, but I know the production cabinet shop next door to me uses a .070-in. tip.

Contact cement is applied the same as any other finish. Good coverage on both pieces being joined is important, so it makes sense to lay down a full, wet coat. Start by spraying along the piece from front to back, then return immediately to the beginning and run the spray gun from left to right, perpendicular to your first set of passes.

Most contact cements are hazardous and quite flammable and require proper protection and ventilation. The vapors created when spraying solvent-based cements are extremely noxious, so if you don't have adequate ventilation you should stick to water-based products. Non-flammable, water-based cements are not as dangerous to work with, but they take longer to dry, especially on warm, humid days.

Most production shops that do a lot of laminate work have a gun that is used only for spraying contact cement, which means keeping it clean is not a matter of life and death. However, small shops don't have that luxury. The gun that sprays solvent-based cement today may be used to spray water-based lacquer tomorrow. If so, it is important to keep your gun clean. Use the solvent recommended by the contact-cement manufacturer, and proceed as described on pp. 144-150. Dried cement is hard to see and has an amazing ability to get into places you'd never expect. If you don't get the gun clean, a small clump of cement may ball up and clog it the next time you use it. The only good thing I can say about cleaning a gun after using contact cement is that if you miss some, it never really hardens and is fairly easy to remove, even days later, with a toothpick or brush.

Sprayed contact cement also has a tendency to settle on everything in the area, including the spray-booth filters and exhaust fan blades. The sticky, fuzzy overspray is harder to clean than regular finishing materials and will clog your filters quickly. If you spray contact cement, pay close attention to your exhaust fan. The buildup that gathers on the blades gets heavy and may strain the motor. I once had a wall-mounted fan seize up after only one day of spraying water-based contact cement.

**Sprayable contact cements make short work of large lamination jobs. They come in both solvent-based and water-based forms.**

# CHAPTER 8
# Cleaning Up

The first time I used my own spray equipment I was somewhat mystified about the best way to get everything clean, so I simply ran a few ounces of solvent through the gun and put it back in the box. The next time I began spraying I couldn't understand why a brand-new gun that had worked perfectly a few days earlier was suddenly difficult to use. The latex paint I was spraying would not come out of the gun in a full, even pattern. After a few minutes, the gun began to sputter and the paint was shooting out in big blobs. Before I called the manufacturer to demand a refund I decided to take the gun apart to see if there was some obvious solution to the problem. Perhaps the dry paint stuck to the needle and lining the fluid tip had something to do with it?

This time I spent more than a few minutes giving the gun a more thorough cleaning. Naturally, once I removed the dried paint, the gun worked fine. The dramatic difference between working with a dirty gun and working with a clean one made me realize how important it is to clean the gun well. From then on I began to follow a strict schedule of cleaning all my equipment at the end of the day.

**Keeping your equipment clean is important to successful spraying.**

Cleaning a spray gun may be slow and methodical work, but I have found that following the same routine each time I clean my gun eliminates the chance of missing anything and makes a tedious chore more bearable. In fact, you should view the cleaning process as simply one more step in a complete spray schedule.

**Keeping your air supply clean is as important as keeping dirt out of the gun itself. A few blasts of compressed air will remove dust that could clog the filter of a turbine.**

Thoroughly cleaning spray equipment is not limited to the gun alone; it must also include the filters (see the photo above), either on your turbine or compressed-air lines, and the spray area or booth. Keeping everything clean not only helps eliminate any problems with the gun, but also guarantees that the atomizing air is free of debris and that the working environment is clean and healthy.

If you spray a lot of water-based materials you should have stainless-steel equipment. However, this doesn't mean that if you don't have the right type of gun you cannot spray these finishes, as long as you clean the gun thoroughly when you are done. I have been sending water-based lacquer through a gun that doesn't have stainless-steel parts for over three years and have not noticed any adverse effects. I run a few ounces of denatured alcohol through the gun after it is fully cleaned, which helps keep the gun as dry as possible by removing any water left behind. If you have a compressor, a blast of air is also good for drying out the inside of the gun.

Regardless of the material I have been spraying, the last thing I do is run a few ounces of lacquer thinner through the gun. Lacquer thinner will dissolve anything left by the initial cleaning, including small particles of material that you cannot see. This is especially important when using clear finishes. The gun, cup and air cap may look clean, when in reality there may be a thin film of finish coating everything. A quick rinse and spray with a few ounces of clean lacquer thinner will remove dirt your initial cleaning may have missed.

## Which solvent works best?

Guns are cleaned with solvents, and which solvent you use to clean your cup and gun will depend entirely on the type of material you have been spraying. Usually (but not always), whatever you used as a thinner will act as the cleaning solvent. However, it is a common mistake to refer to thinners as solvents and solvents as thinners when in fact the two may be entirely different. A thinner is used to thin the finish prior to application, while a solvent will dissolve dried finish. In some cases the same material can be used as both a solvent and a thinner for a particular finish. Other times, a solvent may not be an appropriate thinner. Knowing what to use and when to use it are important if you spray several different finish materials. The most commonly used thinners and solvents are lacquer thinner, mineral spirits, turpentine, naphtha, denatured alcohol, water and glycol ether. The chart on p. 142 will help you match the right thinners and solvents with the finish material you are spraying.

### Handling and storing solvents

If you do a lot of spraying, you'll be cleaning your gun a lot too, and you'll need to figure out what to do with the dirty solvent. Working with water-based materials is one way to lessen the problem. Because

| THINNERS AND SOLVENTS FOR COMMONLY SPRAYED FINISHES | | |
|---|---|---|
| Finish | Thinner | Solvent |
| Lacquer | Lacquer thinner | Lacquer thinner, denatured alcohol, glycol ether |
| Shellac | Denatured alcohol | Lacquer thinner, denatured alcohol, glycol ether |
| Varnish, oil and oil-based paint | Mineral spirits, turpentine, naphtha | Methylene chloride (paint thinner) |
| Water-based finishes | Water, glycol ether | Lacquer thinner, denatured alcohol, glycol ether |
| Latex paint | Water | Lacquer thinner |

the solvent is water and the material is nontoxic, you can simply pour them down the drain. However, even if you work strictly with water-based finishes, you will generate small amounts of dirty lacquer thinner. If you spray lacquers or solvent-based materials, you have more of a problem. The amount of mineral spirits or lacquer thinner needed to clean your equipment can be quite large. Storing the waste not only takes up a lot of space but could create fire and health hazards.

When I first began spraying, I wasn't sure about what to do with the dirty solvent; in fact, it hadn't occurred to me that cleaning the gun would create a problem. Fortunately a painter friend of mine, who sprays hundreds of gallons of oil-based products a year, showed me his method for storing dirty mineral spirits. It is a simple system that recycles a great deal of the solvent by using the same cleaner more than once.

When I clean my gun I spray the solvent into a 5-gal. pail that is used solely for that purpose. Once the gun is clean I pour the dirty solvent into a container, such as a coffee can or glass jar, that is clearly marked and has a tight-fitting lid. Once that container is full it takes a place on the shelf beside similar containers. After a while the solids, or "dirt,"

If used (dirty) solvent is left alone long enough, the solids will eventually settle to the bottom. The relatively clean liquid at the top of this jar of lacquer thinner can be reused as a cleaning solvent.

settle to the bottom of the can, leaving relatively clean solvent floating on top (see the photo above). The solvent can then be poured into another clean container, ready for reuse. The solid residue left in the can or jar is relatively safe and can be disposed of quite easily. Where I live, it can be thrown in the garbage; check with the local sanitation officials in your town.

The more a solvent is recycled, the dirtier it becomes, so I use old thinner only as a preliminary cleaner or the first wash, and always follow with a rinse of new solvent. Eventually the can of used solvent will become so dirty that no clean liquid is salvageable. When this happens I pour the entire can into an empty gallon container and drop it off at the local hazardous-waste collection site.

The key to making this system work is keeping track of the various containers of solvent. If you do a lot of spray finishing you may end up with several cans of solvent that are in different conditions of cleanliness. If you spray more than one type of material, you may end up with different kinds of solvents in the containers. So long as you have enough shelf space and keep your containers sealed and well-marked, you should have no problem managing what could otherwise become a real headache.

## Cleaning a spray gun

When cleaning a suction-feed or gravity-feed spray gun, remember that it is easier to remove fresh finish than it is to remove old, dried material. The longer you wait to clean your gun, the harder it will be to get it totally clean. Paint and finish tend to accumulate over time, so if you don't get your gun completely clean the first time you clean it, you will find it that much harder to clean the next time.

As long as you are thorough, getting your equipment clean is not difficult. After you have turned off the air supply, trigger the gun into an empty container to release the air and fluid pressure. If your material container is attached to the gun, check to see if it has a pressure-relief valve that must be opened before taking the lid off the top of the cup. If you don't open this valve, pressurized fluid might spray all over you when you try to remove the lid.

Once pressure has been released from the material container, you can open the lid. Hold the gun above the cup until fluid stops dripping from the tube, and then set the gun aside. I usually hook the handle of the gun over the rim of a bucket to catch any drips.

The first part of the gun that should be cleaned is the material container or cup. Empty any remaining liquid before thoroughly rinsing the cup with clean solvent. It is important to remove all traces of the finish you have just been spraying. Any material left in the cup will have to pass through the gun during the next stage of cleaning, or else it will dry in the container.

Also clean the inside of the cup lid and the gasket that seals the two together (see the photo on the facing page). Some guns have a plastic flange that fits over the fluid tube and covers the inside of the lid. The flange helps eliminate the possibility of finish flowing into the air pas-

**If the rim of the cup and rubber gasket on the lid are not kept clean, they won't form a tight seal, causing the cup to lose pressure or leak material.**

sages if the gun is tipped too far sideways or upside down. Pay special attention to the rubber gasket. If it is neglected it may become hard or brittle and will not create a tight seal between the lid and the cup.

Once the cup is clean you are ready to wash the gun. Fill the material container about a third to a half full with clean solvent and then spray it through the gun into an empty bucket. This will clean out the fluid passages and help loosen some of the buildup on the air cap. You should continue to spray solvent through the gun until it comes out clean, which may mean rinsing and filling the cup more than once.

After you are sure the cup and fluid passages are clean, you can re-move the air cap and clean it with a stiff, solvent-soaked brush. Most gun manufacturers sell cleaning kits that have the proper brush; how-

**A stiff-bristled toothbrush dipped in solvent will remove dried finish without damaging any of a gun's parts.**

**A toothpick is the ideal instrument for picking small specks of dried finish off the precisely machined parts of a spray gun.**

ever, an old toothbrush works just as well (see the photo above left). If the air cap is especially dirty, soak it in clean solvent for a few minutes. What's important here is to be sure that all of the small holes in the air cap are completely free of obstruction. You may have to clean out the holes with a toothpick (see the photo above right) or a straw from a broom. Never use any sharp objects such as nails or wire. They could ruin the air cap by deforming or enlarging the holes, which could, in turn, create an irregular spray pattern.

The last step to cleaning your gun is to wipe off the outside of all the parts with a rag dampened with solvent. Although getting the outside of your gun and cup clean will not directly affect how the gun sprays, it is good to do so anyway. Finish has a way of creeping into places you least expect, so the cleaner you get your gun today, the fewer problems you will have with it tomorrow.

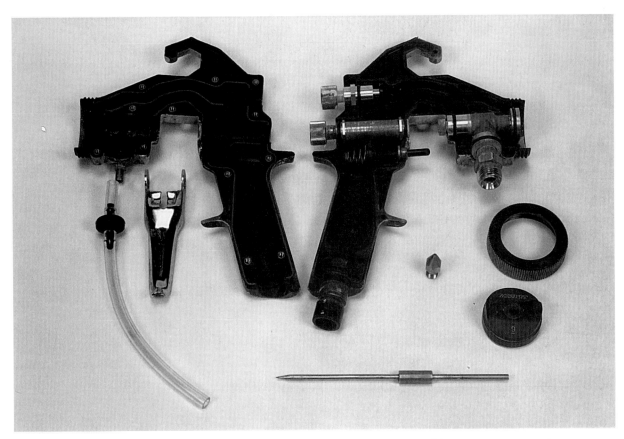

Most guns are easy to disassemble for cleaning. There may be a lot of screws and loose parts, so be careful to account for everything as you take the gun apart.

Once everything is fully cleaned, place the air cap back on the gun and attach the lid to the cup. Your gun should always be stored with the air cap in place because it will protect the fluid tip from damage if the gun is dropped or banged against something. Likewise, putting the lid back on the cup will protect the inside from damage and will help keep out contaminants such as dirt, oil or dust.

If your gun is extremely dirty, you may have to disassemble it (see the photo above) and clean each part individually. Lacquer thinner will remove dried finish quite easily, although you may have to soak the part for a few hours. If you have to take the gun apart to clean the inner workings, be sure to remove any rubber gaskets or O-rings first. If they are left soaking in lacquer thinner for even a short time, they will swell and expand (see the photo on p. 148). Eventually they will return to their normal shape, but until they do, you won't be able to use your gun. Lacquer thinner also removes the oils that keep an O-ring flexible. Soaking makes them brittle over time and prone to breakage.

**Never let your rubber gaskets or O-rings soak in solvent. A mere ten-minute soak in lacquer thinner has caused the ring at right to swell significantly as compared to the normal ring at left.**

Even though most guns come with a parts diagram, these are often unclear or confusing. The first time you take your gun apart, pay careful attention to where each piece goes. This will make reassembly much easier. Also, you should always be careful when handling the fluid tip and needle. These are precision machined and could easily be ruined if dropped on a hard surface.

## Cleaning a pressure-feed system

The procedure for cleaning a pressure-feed system is very similar to that used with a suction or gravity-feed gun. The main difference is that you must get the fluid lines clean as well. The easiest way to do this is to blow the finish material through the lines back into the material container (see the photo on the facing page).

First, be sure the air that pressurizes the fluid is turned off and the lid to the pressure pot is loose. Next, loosen the air-cap retaining ring a turn or two and place a rag tightly against the front of the air cap. Triggering the atomizing air will force any fluid in the lines back into the material tank.

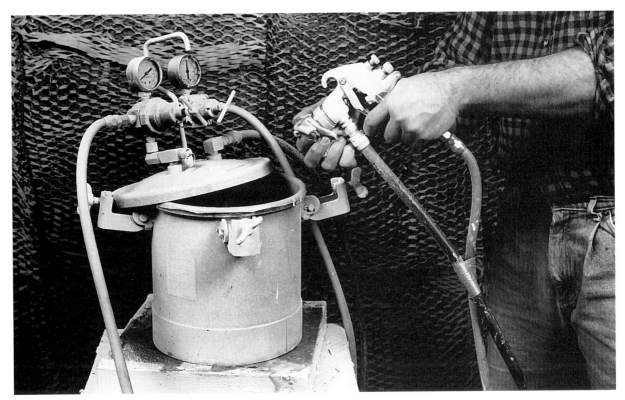

**Before cleaning the gun on a pressure-feed system, blow any remaining finish back through the fluid line into the pressure pot.**

Once the fluid lines have been purged, you can follow the same steps you would for cleaning any other gun. The fluid container must be thoroughly cleaned, followed by the gun itself. After you spray the solvent through the system, you should be sure to blow back any remaining material into the pressure tank as described above; otherwise, you may have solvent sitting in your fluid hoses, waiting to make an appearance on the surface of the next project you spray.

## Gun and hose cleaners

If you do a lot of spray finishing and have several guns and lines operating on a heavy schedule, you may want to use gun and hose cleaners to speed up daily maintenance. A gun cleaner, or washer, is an enclosed structure similar to a dishwasher. Guns and cups are set on top of nozzles inside the washer, and pressurized solvent is sprayed through the nozzles to clean the equipment. The dirty solvent is fully contained and can be drained for proper disposal.

A hose cleaner attached to the fluid line forces a highly turbulent mixture of pressurized air and solvent through the hose and gun. The precisely measured combination of air and solvent acts to scrub the inside of the fluid hose, removing residual finish material. Hose cleaners are easy and fast and reduce the amount of solvent needed to clean the fluid lines effectively; however, unless you plan on doing a lot of spraying, it's hard to justify the expense of gun and hose cleaners.

## Gun lubrication

In order for a spray gun to function properly it must be clean and lubricated regularly. Otherwise it will eventually begin to stick, drip, bind and generally become difficult to use. For this reason, a gun should be lubricated after every cleaning. Each time you clean your gun you wash away the oil that cushions the various friction points, so it is important that the lubricant be replaced.

Anything that moves or has threads needs to be lubricated each time you use your gun. As shown in the drawing on the facing page, this includes the air- and fluid-adjustment knobs on the back of the gun, the trigger bearing screw, the fluid-needle spring and the air-valve rod and trigger. Also hit the fluid-needle packing with a few drops of oil now and then to help keep it soft. If the packing is left without lubrication for too long, it will become dry and hard and may cause the fluid needle to bind or leak.

The type or brand of lubricant you use should be designed for spray guns and contain no silicone. Silicones are a contaminant that will ruin your sprayed finish by creating fisheye (see pp. 108-109). Once silicone gets into your gun it is extremely difficult to get rid of, so under

**Although there are lubricants made specifically for spray guns, petroleum jelly works just as well.**

## Lubrication Points

*To minimize wear and maximize performance, you should lubricate your gun after every cleaning at the points indicated. In addition, the fluid-needle packing should be given an occasional drop of oil to help keep it from becoming dry or hard.*

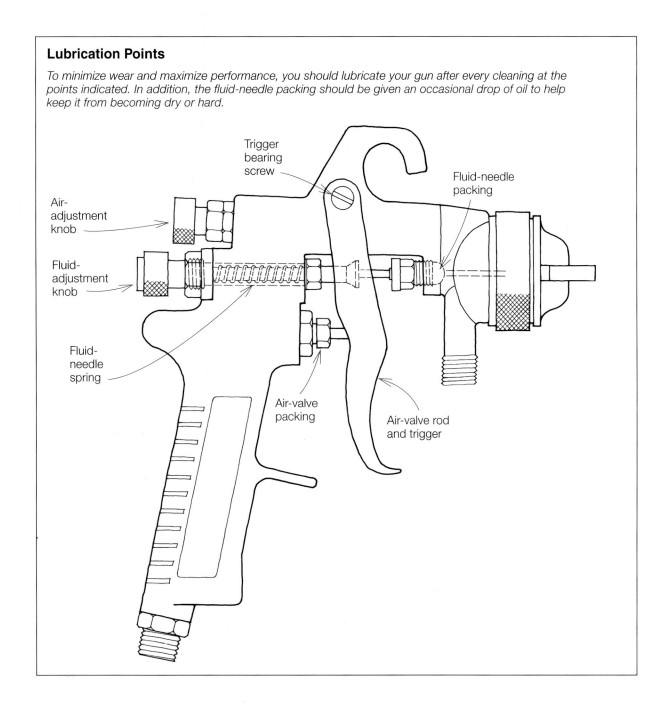

no circumstances should you use a lubricant that contains it. The store that sold you your spray equipment will probably offer some type of maintenance kit. These kits usually contain a wrench, cleaning brushes and a tube of lubricant. Petroleum jelly makes a good substitute for spray-gun lubricant and works just as well.

# TROUBLESHOOTING

It's not unusual to need to tinker with your spray-gun setup, finishes and application techniques to achieve optimum results. The following charts list the problems you are most likely to encounter with spray equipment (pp. 152-154) and with materials and application techniques (pp. 155-157), along with their causes and solutions.

| EQUIPMENT | | |
|---|---|---|
| **Problem** | **Cause** | **Solution** |
| Leaky packing nut | Packing nut is too loose. | Tighten packing nut until fluid stops leaking. If the nut is too tight, the needle will bind. |
| | Packing nut is worn out or too dry. | Lubricate the packing. If this doesn't work, the packing needs to be replaced. |
| Air escaping from front of gun (nonbleed guns) | Air valve in trigger is stuck, worn or misaligned. | Try cleaning and lubricating the stem first. If this doesn't work, you may have to replace the stem, valve, spring or gasket. |
| Fluid leaking from front of gun | Packing nut is too tight. | Loosen until needle moves freely. |
| | Packing is worn or dry. | Lubricate or replace packing. |
| | Fluid-needle spring is missing or broken. | Replace fluid-needle spring. |
| | Dried finish or dirt is in fluid tip. | Clean fluid tip. |
| | Needle and tip are mismatched. | Replace with correct combination. |
| | Fluid tip and/or needle are damaged. | Replace with new needle and/or tip. |
| | Fluid tip is loose. | Tighten fluid tip. |
| Fluid leaking from cup | Dirty or worn gasket creates poor seal. | Clean or replace gasket. |
| | Cup and/or lid are damaged. | Replace cup or lid. |

| Problem | Cause | Solution |
|---|---|---|
| Spray pattern heavy on the top, bottom, left or right. | Obstruction or buildup of finish on air cap or inside fluid tip. | First determine whether problem is with air cap or fluid tip by making a test spray and then rotating air cap 180°. If air cap is plugged, the spray pattern will be reversed. If obstruction is in fluid tip, the pattern will be the same. Once location of problem is found, clean air cap or tip. |
| Center-heavy spray pattern | Material flow or pressure is too high for air cap. | Thin material or decrease fluid flow. |
| | Fan pattern is too small. | Increase size of fan pattern. |
| | Material is too heavy. | Add thinner to material. |
| Split spray pattern | There is not enough fluid. | Increase fluid flow by backing out fluid adjustment knob. |
| | Atomization pressure is too high. | Lower air pressure at regulator (pressure-feed systems). Use larger air cap (turbine systems). |
| | Fluid pressure is not high enough (pressure-feed systems only). | Increase fluid pressure. |
| Starved spray pattern | There is insufficient material flow. | Increase fluid flow. |
| | Fluid hose is dirty or clogged (pressure-feed systems only). | Clean or replace hose. |
| | Fluid tip is too small. | Change to larger tip. |
| Gun will not spray | Fluid tip is too small or clogged. | Change to bigger tip or clean fluid tip. |
| | There is loss of air pressure in cup or pot. | Check gasket for tight seal. |
| | Fluid tube or hose is clogged. | Clean fluid tube or hose. |
| | No air or fluid pressure is available. | Check air lines, hoses, compressor or turbine. |
| | Fluid is too thick to spray. | Thin fluid to proper viscosity. |

| Problem | Cause | Solution |
|---------|-------|----------|
| Pulsating spray | Material container is low on fluid. | Fill with more finish material. |
| | Packing is loose, dry or worn. | Tighten, lubricate or replace packing. |
| | Fluid tip is loose or damaged. | Tighten or replace fluid tip. |
| | Fluid tube or hose is blocked. | Clean fluid tube or hose. |
| | Material is too thick. | Thin material to proper viscosity. |
| | Vent in suction-feed cup is plugged. | Clean vent. |
| | Gun is tipped too far, or is upside down. | Rotate fluid tube so it is pointed toward back of cup. |
| Cannot form round spray pattern | Fan-adjustment knob is broken or not installed properly. | Replace knob or reinstall. |
| Insufficient air pressure | Filters on compressed-air lines or turbine are dirty or clogged. | Clean or replace filters. |
| | Air hose is too small (pressure-feed systems). | Install larger-diameter hose. |
| | Air hose is too long to maintain sufficient pressure (pressure drop). | Shorten hose. |
| Air pressure too high (compressed-air systems) | Regulator is malfunctioning or broken. | Clean or replace regulator. |

# MATERIALS AND APPLICATION TECHNIQUES

| Problem | Cause | Solution |
|---|---|---|
| Excessive overspray, dry spray | Atomization air pressure is too high. | Decrease pressure (compressed-air systems) or use larger air cap (turbine systems). |
| | Gun is held too far from surface. | Hold gun closer to surface. |
| | Gun is moving too fast. | Slow motion to achieve wetter coat. |
| | Material is too thick to atomize properly or contains so much thinner that it dries too fast. | Adjust material to proper viscosity. |
| Runs, sags, drips | Finish is going on too thick. | Reduce fluid flow and/or decrease size of fluid tip. |
| | Material is too thin. | Use less thinner. |
| | Gun is too close to surface. | Move gun back. |
| | Gun is being moved too slowly. | Increase hand speed. |
| | Gun is tipped at an angle. | Hold gun perpendicular to target. |
| | Improper triggering. | Start motion before gun is triggered and release trigger before end of motion. |
| Orange peel | There is insufficient atomization. | Increase air pressure (compressed-air systems) or install smaller air cap (turbine-driven systems). |
| | Material is too thick. | Thin material to proper viscosity. |
| | Material is drying too fast. | Use proper thinner or move gun closer to surface. |
| | Coat is sprayed too thin. | Increase fluid flow or slow down hand motion. |

| Problem | Cause | Solution |
|---|---|---|
| Solvent pop | Trapped solvent breaking through surface of fast-drying finish | Slow down dry time by lowering temperature of finishing area. |
| | Too much thinner has been added to material. | Add more material to increase ratio of material to thinner. |
| | Coats applied too heavily or quickly | Reduce material flow; allow more drying time between coats. |
| | Wrong thinner is being used. | Use thinner recommended by manufacturer. |
| Pinholes in the surface of the finish (especially solvent-based finishes) | Coat has been applied too heavily. | Spray lighter coats or add more thinner to material. |
| | Surface preparation is inadequate on open-pored wood. | Use pore filler or spray sealer to close open pores. |
| Finish cracks or blisters | There is moisture on surface. | Clean and dry surface. |
| | Coatings are not compatible. | Change coatings or use sealer between coats. |
| | Wrong thinner is being used. | Use thinner recommended by manufacturer. |
| | Coats have been applied too heavily. | Spray lighter coats. |
| | Coats are not being allowed to dry. | Allow more time between coats. |
| | Temperature of finish or surface being sprayed is too low. | Increase temperature in finishing room. Do not store finish materials on a concrete floor, especially in winter. Be sure finish and surface being sprayed are same temperature. |

| Problem | Cause | Solution |
|---|---|---|
| Fisheye (see pp. 110-112) | There is oil, wax or silicone on wood surface. | Thoroughly clean surface with mineral spirits and apply sealer. Spray several light mist coats over contaminated area. Add recommended fisheye eliminator to finish. |
| | Gun is contaminated with oil. | Clean gun. Use only silicone-free lubricants. Clean or install separator on compressed-air line. |
| Blush (see p. 112) | There is water in spray equipment or finish material. | Use compressed air or alcohol to dry equipment. Clean or install water separator in compressed air line. |
| | Humidity is too high. | Use dehumidifier in shop. Add blush retarder to finish. Wait for a drier day to spray. |
| Bumpy, coarse surface | There is dirt or dust in finish. | Remove all dust from air in finishing room. Thoroughly wipe down surface being sprayed with damp rag. |
| | Material is contaminated or old. | Strain material or use fresh material. |
| Mottled or textured surface (especially water-based finishes and latex paint) | Coats are applied too heavily. | Spray thinner coats by reducing fluid flow or increasing arm speed. |
| | Material is too thin. | Use less thinner. |
| | Gun is being held too close to surface, causing finish to ripple or move. | Hold gun farther from surface; decrease air pressure (compressed-air systems). |
| Microbubbles form in finish, clouding or obscuring underlying surface (water-based finishes) | Material is atomized too finely. | Decrease atomizing air pressure (compressed-air systems); use larger air cap (turbine-driven systems). |
| | Material is drying too fast. | Add recommended retarder. |
| Finish looks bland or washed out (water-based finishes) | Inherent clarity characteristic of many water-based finishes. | Add tiny amount of red or brown tint to finish; spray wash coat of dewaxed shellac first. |

# SPRAY SCHEDULES

Once I have a routine that works well for a particular process, I write down the sequence of operations in a spray schedule that becomes the basis for future jobs. The three given here are for water-based lacquer top coat over water-based dye, water-based lacquer top coat over pigmented stain, and pigmented lacquer. These schedules are provided as examples of the steps involved with spraying different types of finishes. They are intended to serve as starting points as you develop your own schedules.

## Water-based dye and water-based lacquer top coat

This is a typical schedule for spraying a piece that is finished with a water-based dye and a clear, water-based lacquer top coat. The drying times are for the specific brand of lacquer I use, sprayed on a day with low humidity, and are shown as relative guidelines. The amount of time you allow between coats will vary according to the brand of material and the surrounding conditions. Best results are obtained through a combination of following the manufacturer's recommendations and using your own judgment. If a coat of finish feels soft or can be dented with a fingernail, it is probably not dry enough to sand. If the sandpaper gums up quickly with streaks and blobs of finish, you should wait. If the sandpaper creates a fine dust or powder, the finish is dry enough to sand.

Under ideal conditions my schedule can usually be completed in one day. Conditions are seldom ideal though, and water-based finishes are very sensitive to humidity, so this schedule frequently stretches over two days.

Between coats, always wipe down the piece with a slightly moist cloth to remove any dust. Never use tack cloths with water-based finishes because they will leave behind sticky residue that will attract dust, dirt or fingerprints and will show through the finish. Also, steel wool should not be used when spraying water-based finishes. Small particles can become lodged in the wood and will react with the finish, leaving behind black marks that may not be noticeable until well after the piece is done. The schedule I use is as follows:

1. Sand item to 180 grit.

2. Lightly mist piece with water using a plastic spray bottle and sand with 220 grit when dry (usually 10 min. to 15 min.)

3. Spray on light coat of dye and sand with 320 grit when dry (usually 30 min. to 60 min.), trying to cut through the dye as little as possible.

4. Spray on second, slightly heavier coat of dye to cover any cut-through from sanding and to even out color. Allow to dry for about one hour.

5. Spray on fairly light wash coat of 1-lb cut clear shellac that has been dewaxed (see p. 115).

6. Let dry, again for about one hour, then sand with 400-grit paper.

7. Spray on first, fairly light coat of lacquer. Let dry for about two hours. Once the piece is dry, some sanding may be necessary, but if your preparation and application have been good you may not have to sand again until after the final coat, and sometimes not even then.

8. Spray second coat of lacquer. If all is going well and you don't need to do any sanding, you can spray the third and any additional coats of lacquer in 30-min. to 60-min. intervals.

9. Let the finish dry completely before sanding with 400-grit to 600-grit paper or rubbing out to the desired gloss. I let a finished piece dry at least several hours, depending on how many coats of lacquer I sprayed and how pressed I am for time, but ideally it should be allowed to dry overnight. Often, a good spray job will not even need a final sanding, but this depends on the type and quality of finish desired.

# Pigmented stain and water-based lacquer top coat

Although you will hear it said that you should never combine solvent- and water-based products, I do it all the time. The key to making this method work is to insert a layer of material between the two finishes that will seal and separate them and act as a bonding agent. There are sealers designed for this purpose, but I have had mixed results with some of them. Instead, I use dewaxed shellac between the two otherwise incompatible products. The results are consistent: It has always worked. The spray schedule I use in these situations is as follows:

1. Sand piece to 220 grit.

2. Apply stain with brush or rag, wiping off excess.

3. Spray wash coat of 1-lb. cut, dewaxed shellac. The shellac seals the stain and helps the dissimilar water-based and oil-based mixtures bond.

4. Spray on first coat of lacquer and let dry for one to two hours (depending on weather conditions, this process may take longer), and sand with 320-grit wet/dry paper.

5. Wipe off sanding dust with slightly damp rag. Never use tack cloths with water-based finishes. They leave behind an oily residue that attracts dust and fingerprints and will clearly show through the finish.

6. Apply subsequent coats of lacquer. I usually apply as few as two and as many as four, depending on the intended use of the piece and desired quality of finish. If the surface has been properly prepared and sanded after the first coat, additional sanding should be light and only needed to remove dust.

7. Water-based products do not rub out to a gloss finish very well, so I often leave them alone once the final coat has been applied. However, they buff to a satin finish quite nicely with some fine rubbing compound or 600-grit wet/dry sandpaper. Never use steel wool on wood being finished with water-based products. Small particles left behind become trapped in the finish and rust, leaving black marks buried in the surface.

# Pigmented lacquer

Although this schedule was developed for spraying pigmented lacquers, it will work equally well for spraying latex or oil-based paint. The only adjustment you will need to make when using paint is to increase the drying time allowed between coats.

1. After all defects and nail holes have been filled with putty, sand the entire piece to 120 grit.

2. Spray on coat of primer.

3. Fill all defects highlighted by primer and sand with 220-grit wet/dry paper, avoiding cut-through as much as possible.

4. Spray on second coat of primer.

5. If necessary, repeat step 3; otherwise, sand primer with 320-grit wet/dry paper. At this point the surface should be perfectly smooth and ready for the color coats. If not, repeat step 3 as many times as necessary to obtain a flawlessly smooth surface.

6. Spray on first coat of pigmented lacquer.

7. Sand with 400-grit wet/dry paper if necessary to remove dust or other blemishes.

8. Spray subsequent coat(s) of lacquer until desired depth of finish is achieved.

9. If the piece being finished requires extra protection, or if you want to alter the gloss or depth of the finish, at this point, spray on one or more coats of an appropriate clear finish, sanding between coats only if necessary.

10. Rub out or buff final coat.

# GLOSSARY

**Air-assisted airless**
An airless system that has pressurized air mixed with the fluid as it is pumped through the tip of the gun.

**Air cap**
The removable cap at the tip of a spray gun that atomizes the finish material by directing pressurized air into a fluid stream.

**Airless**
A type of spray system where fluid is forced through the tip of a gun by a pump.

**Annular hole**
The center hole in an air cap through which atomizing air is introduced into the fluid stream.

**Atomization**
The process whereby fluid is broken into tiny particles by pressurized air.

**Bench booth**
A spray booth with a built-in bench or countertop.

**Bleeder gun**
A spray gun that has air continuously moving through the tip of the gun.

**Blush**
A hazy film that forms as droplets of water are trapped beneath the drying finish.

**Bounce back**
Tiny particles of atomized finish material that bounce off the target surface back toward the spray gun.

**Bypass turbine**
A turbine that has separate air-intake and cooling fans.

**Coalescer**
A filter unit attached to compressed-air lines that removes tiny contaminants by sending the air through microfibers of borosilicate glass.

**Conversion gun**
A compressed-air spray gun that has a regulator that converts the gun to an HVLP system.

**Cotton blush**
Tiny, cotton-like particles that appear on the surface of a lacquer finish, usually caused by moisture or use of the wrong type of lacquer thinner.

**Crawl**
A wrinkled film formed when wet finish is moved or pushed across the surface by air pressure; usually caused by a combination of applying too heavy a coat and holding the gun too close to the surface.

**Cup**
The material container used with a spray gun. Typical size ranges from 4 oz. to 2 qt.

**Cut-through**
A flaw caused by sanding away too much of the finish, revealing the bare wood underneath; commonly occurs on sharp edges and corners.

**Dewaxing**
The process whereby naturally occurring wax is removed from shellac.

**Dryer**
A filter unit attached to compressed-air lines containing chemical desiccants used to reduce the amount of water in the air below the dew point.

**Dry spray**
Tiny particles of finish that dry before they hit the surface being sprayed (also called overspray). Can be caused by too much thinner, too much atomization pressure or by holding the gun too far from the target.

**Electrostatic spray**
A system where the finish material is attracted to the surface being sprayed by opposing electrical charges.

**External-mix air cap**
A cap that mixes air and fluid outside of the tip of the gun.

**Feathering**
The process where the amount of finish applied to a certain area is controlled by a combination of a light touch on the spray gun's trigger and a quick, sweeping wrist motion.

**Fisheye**
Small, circular spots or holes in a finish, usually caused by oil, wax or silicone contamination in the equipment or on the surface being sprayed.

**Flash off**
The process whereby fast-drying solvents are quickly released or evaporate out of a freshly sprayed finish.

**Floor booth**
A large, walk-in spray booth.

**Gravity feed**
A spray gun that uses gravity to force fluid from the cup to the tip of the gun; easily recognized by the position of the material container, which is mounted on top of the gun.

**Horns**
The two holes that project from the perimeter of an air cap that are used to control the fan pattern of the material being sprayed.

**HVLP (high volume, low pressure)**
A spray system that uses large amounts of relatively slow-moving air to atomize fluid. Can be either compressor or turbine driven.

**Internal-mix air cap**
An air cap that combines atomizing air and fluid inside the tip of the gun before forcing the liquid through a single opening.

**Manometer, or draft gauge**
A device that measures air pressure moving into the exhaust chamber of a spray booth; used to indicate when filters need to be changed.

**Microbubbles**
Microscopic bubbles that become trapped in the surface of a drying finish, giving it a white or hazy look. A common problem with water-based finishes.

**Nonbleed gun**
A spray gun that contains a valve in the trigger mechanism that, when released, shuts off air flow through the gun.

**Non-grain-raising (NGR) dye**
A type of water-soluble dye that comes premixed with solvents, including alcohol and lacquer thinner, which help reduce the grain-raising properties of the dye.

**Orange peel**
A problem commonly associated with all types of spray equipment and material, in which the fluid does not flow together properly, forming a rough, bumpy surface that resembles the skin of an orange.

**Overspray**
Atomized material that either dries before it has a chance to coat the surface being finished (also called dry spray) or misses the target completely, filling the air surrounding the workpiece.

**Peripheral turbine**
An HVLP turbine that draws air in through one end and releases it into an exhaust collar, which then channels the air to a hose outlet.

**Pinholes**

Tiny bubbles that appear in a finished surface, caused by material trapped in the pores of the wood making its way to the already dried surface; usually occur in open-grained woods like oak or mahogany.

**Poppet, or check valve**

A relief mechanism on a material container that, when opened, allows pressure in the container to escape.

**Pressure feed**

A spray system that uses positive pressure in a fluid cup or container to move material to the tip of the gun.

**Rubbing out**

The use of a combination of fine sandpaper, steel wool and polishing compounds to give a finished surface its final luster.

**Separator**

A filter unit attached to compressed-air lines that removes particles of dirt and water by swirling incoming air through a chamber before passing it out the other side.

**Shading**

Using a mix of tinted or colored finish to highlight certain areas of a piece.

**Siphon (suction) feed**

A spray system that moves fluid into the atomizing air stream by creating a vacuum at the tip of the gun.

**Solvent**

Any material that will dissolve a dried finish.

**Solvent pop**

Tiny, pin-prick bubbles that appear in a finish as excessive amounts of thinner work their way through the surface of a finish that has already dried or skinned over.

**Spatter finish**

The spray technique of applying a small amount of solvent over a still-wet painted surface; used to reveal the color of the base coat while giving the surface a textured or patterned look.

**Stage**

A fan or compression chamber in a turbine. Turbines are rated according to the number of fans, or stages, they have.

**Tangential turbine**

A turbine that directs air through its stages into an air outlet, or horn, on the side of the motor.

**Thinner**

A liquid that is added to a finish to lower its viscosity or alter its drying time.

**Thru-flow turbine**

A turbine that uses the same fan for compression and cooling.

**Toning**

The act of applying a tinted or colored coat of finish over an entire piece.

**Touch-up booth**

A small spray booth that sits on metal legs or on top of a workbench; usually used for spraying small parts.

**Viscosity**

A measure of the thickness of a fluid based on the internal friction of the molecules of liquid as they flow past each other.

**Viscosity cup**

A small container with a hole in the bottom used to measure the thickness of a liquid. Timing how long it takes for the fluid to drain through the cup helps determine if the liquid needs to be thinned for spraying and how much thinner to add.

**Volatile organic compounds (VOCs)**

The hydrocarbons found in solvents that, when released into the air, react with sunlight to form smog.

**Waterwash**

A type of spray booth that uses a curtain of water to filter and trap overspray.

**Witness lines**

Faint marks or shadows that appear when a finish is sanded or cut through, revealing an underlying layer of finish.

**Worthy screens**

Small filters placed directly into the end of a fluid tube.

# INDEX

**Editor:** RUTH DOBSEVAGE

**Designer/Layout Artist:** AMY L. BERNARD

**Illustrator:** VINCE BABAK

**Photographer, except where noted:**
CHIP CAROSIA / EINROSIA PHOTOGRAPHY



**Typeface:** GARAMOND

**Paper:** MOISTRITE, 70 LB., NEUTRAL pH

**Printer:** QUEBECOR PRINTING / HAWKINS,
NEW CANTON, TENNESSEE